Competition

How to Speak Like an Expert

Emmanuel Combe

Foreword by Laurence Boone

Concurrences, 2023

Titre original : *La Concurrrence - 2e édition augmentée*
Copyright © Presses Universitaires de France/Humensis, 2022

Pour la traduction anglaise :
Copyright © 2023 by Institute of Competition Law
106 West 32nd Street, Suite 144 New York, NY, 10001, USA
www.concurrences.com
book@concurrences.com

First Printing, September 2023
978-1-939007-35-3 (Paperback)
Library of Congress Control Number: 2023944505

Cover Design : Yves Buliard, www.yvesbuliard.fr
Book Design and Layout implementation: Nord Compo

Concurrences Books

Tributes

Eleanor M. Fox – Antitrust Ambassador
to the World, *2021*

Herbert Hovenkamp – The Dean of American
Antitrust Law, *2021*

Frédéric Jenny – Standing Up for Convergence and
Relevance in Antitrust, (Vol. I & II), *2019 & 2021*

Albert Foer – A Consumer Voice in the Antitrust
Arena, *2020*

Richard Whish – Taking Competition Law Outside
the Box, *2020*

Douglas H. Ginsburg – An Antitrust Professor
on the Bench (Vol. I & II), *2018 & 2020*

Wang Xiaoye – The Pioneer of Competition Law in
China, *A. Emch, W. Ng (eds.), 2019*

Ian S. Forrester – A Scot without Borders
(Vol. I & II), *A. Komninos (eds.), 2015*

William E. Kovacic – An Antitrust Tribute
(Vol. I & II), *2013 & 2014*

Practical Books

Global Dictionary of Competition Law, *D. Healey,
W. Kovacic, P. Trevisan, R. Whish, 2023*

Antitrust in Life Sciences, *M. Cowie, G. Gordon,
M. Thill-Tayara, 2023*

State Aid & the Energy Transition, *D. Buschle,
L. Hancher, M.-T. Richter-Kuhnert (eds.), 2023
(in collaboration with the Energy Community)*

State Aid & National Enforcement, *J. Derenne,
D. Jouve, C. Lemaire, F. Martucci (eds.), 2023*

Antitrust and the Digital Economy, *Y. Katsoulacos
(ed.), 2023 (in collaboration with CRESSE)*

Judicial Review of Competition Cases, *D. Ginsburg,
T. Eicke (eds.), 2023*

Competition Law Treatment of Joint Ventures,
*B. Bleicher, N. Campbell, A. Hamilton,
N. Hukkinen, A. Khan, A. Mordaunt (eds.), 2022
(in collaboration with the IBA)*

Information Exchange & Related Risks, *Z. Marosi,
M. Soares (eds.), 2022 (in collaboration with the IBA)*

Rulemaking Authority of the US Federal Trade
Commission, *D. Crane (ed.), 2022*

The International Competition Network at Twenty,
D. Anderson & P. Lugard (eds.), 2022

Competition Case Law Digest – 5th Edition,
F. Jenny, N. Charbit (eds.), 2022

Competition Inspections in 21 Jurisdictions –
A Practitioner's Guide, *N. Jalabert-Doury (ed.), 2022*

Perspectives on Antitrust Compliance, *A. Riley,
A. Stephan, A. Tubbs (eds.), 2022 (in collaboration
with the ICC)*

Turkish Competition Law, *G. Gürkaynak, 2021*

Competition Law – Climate Change &
Environmental Sustainability, *S. Holmes,
D. Middelschulte, M. Snoep (eds.), 2021*

Merger Control in Latin America – A Jurisdictional
Guide, *P. Burnier da Silveira, P. Sittenfeld (eds.), 2020*

Competition Inspections under EU Law –
A Practitioner's Guide, *N. Jalabert-Doury, 2020*

Gun Jumping in Merger Control – A Jurisdictional
Guide, *C. Hatton, Y. Comtois, A. Hamilton (eds.),
2019 (in collaboration with the IBA)*

Choice – A New Standard for Competition
Analysis? *P. Nihoul (ed.), 2016*

PhD Theses

Abuse of Platform Power, *F. Bostoen, 2023*

Reform of Chinese State-Owned Enterprises,
X. Bai, 2023

Competition & Regulation in Network Industries –
Essays in Industrial Organization, *J-M. Zogheib, 2021*

The Role of Media Pluralism in the Enforcement
of EU Competition Law, *K. Bania, 2019*

Buyer Power, *I. Herrera Anchustegui, 2017*

General Interest

Women and Antitrust – Voices from the Field (Vol I
& II), *E. Kurgonaite & K. Nordlander, 2020*

Conference Proceedings

Antitrust in Emerging and Developing Countries –
(Vol I & II), *E. Fox, H. First, 2015 & 2016*

Global Antitrust Law – Current Issues
in Antitrust Law and Economics, *D. Ginsburg,
J. Wright, (eds.) 2015*

Competition Law on the Global Stage – David
Gerber's Global Competition Law in Perspective,
D. Gerber, 2014

e-Book versions available for
Concurrences+ subscribers

For Aurélien and Floriane.
For Sylvie.

"It is competition that puts a just price on goods
and establishes the true relations between them"
Montesquieu, *De l'esprit des lois* (1748)*

---

*   Translated by Cohler, Miller and Stone (Cambridge University Press, 17th ed., 2013).

Table of contents

I

III

Foreword

LAURENCE BOONE
Secretary of State for European Affairs

Competition is sometimes perceived as a strong incentive, sometimes denounced for its harshness. It is part of the criticism of globalization. Very often, as consumers, we welcome it. As employees we fear it, and as citizens we doubt its validity. Who has not once protested against a firm that does not play by the same rules as the others? Who, on the other hand, has not been pleased to see prices fall or quality improvement after a new firm enters the market?

To get away from these two polar views – both of which contain some truth but do not reflect the subject in its entirety – it is useful to call on economics, a social science that, since Adam Smith's *Wealth of Nations* (1776), has devoted a great deal of attention to competition and its effects. Of course, like any science, economics is and will continue to be the subject of debate and controversy. But it has the merit of providing a rigorous analytical framework for thinking about competition in all of its dimensions, with hypotheses and conclusions that we can empirically test. And above all, economics has the ability to design good practices that maximize the benefits and correct the negative side effects of competition.

It is in this reasoned and objective way that Emmanuel Combe's book, unique in its kind, fits.

In keeping with academic tradition, Combe's book is more demonstrative than affirmative. Combe does not assert truths; he works to explain, support, and even "deconstruct" all of the economic mechanisms of competition, and he does so as an honest man. The analysis of the effects of competition on employment illustrates this perfectly.

Competition is often perceived as a vector of job destruction, an effect that Combe acknowledges. But further exploring the global functioning of the economy, he shows that limiting the analysis to this first and direct effect would be incomplete: competition also has indirect and positive effects on employment. The merit of this book is that it does not stop at a partial vision. It shows how competition plays out in all sectors of the economy, bringing to light what is sometimes little or not visible to us.

Emmanuel Combe is anything but a competition ideologue. He considers competition first and foremost as a tool – a tool that can stimulate growth, employment, productivity, and innovation, but that can also have undesirable effects. He shows us, however, that we should not give up on competition when it is useful and beneficial. And he points out that it is imperative to frame competition with a set of appropriate economic policies so that it benefits the greatest number of people, without leaving anyone by the wayside. Combe, who was also vice-chairman of the French Competition Authority for ten years (2012–2022), delivers an essential message here: competition implies rules; it is not the law of the jungle but that of the most deserving. Alongside formative and continuing education, investment, and innovation, competition can be a formidable ingredient of economic growth and social justice – if it is governed by rules and institutions. This is why, Combe contends, competition policy should play a key role in preventing and punishing illegal cartels and abuses of dominant positions. It is probably no coincidence that more than 130 countries in the world now have competition laws. Similarly, Combe shows us that developed countries still have room for pro-competitive reforms that will improve productivity, growth, and, above all, employment, as shown in particular by the OECD's studies. He rightly points out the institutional and political obstacles to such reforms, whose gains are long-term and diffuse while their costs are more immediate and visible. He stresses that these costs should not be denied, but that redistributive policies should be instituted to support those affected by these immediate negative effects.

Intellectually demanding, this book is also and above all educational: Emmanuel Combe excels at making sometimes complex concepts accessible to all and giving an exhaustive vision of the various facets of competition. This book is rooted in reality and full of concrete examples and empirical studies, whether regarding the entry of new operators in a sector, competition from imports, or the opening up of network industries to competition. Far from relying solely on proven knowledge, Combe does not hesitate to mobilize more recent and original contributions from economic science – in particular, the fact that consumer bias can attenuate competition in a market.

The examples he uses, and his understanding of the behavior of individuals and firms, make this book not only accessible, but also easy to read. Readers will finish this book with a fuller comprehension of Cournot's oligopoly, "contestable markets," natural monopoly, and network effects – and will be better able to look at concrete cases with an objective understanding.

This book is a remarkable work of explanation and demonstration, which should enable world citizens and decision-makers to be better informed. This exercise in education seems to me to be more essential today than ever: if we want competition to remain a precious tool for growth, it is imperative that we explain its meaning, that we understand it in all its effects, and that we make the keys to its understanding accessible.

Acknowledgments

Although writing a book is primarily a solitary exercise, I would like to warmly thank Sylvie Cognet, Denis Ferrand, Thomas Piquereau, Umberto Berkani, and Anne Wachsmann for their proofreading and valuable advice.

I am also very grateful to Laurence Boone, Secretary of State for European Affairs, for agreeing to preface this book.

I am, of course, solely responsible for any errors that may remain.

Introduction

The public perception of competition is often ambivalent.

Some people see it as a strong incentive for individuals and firms that allows the most deserving to showcase their talents. Accordingly, the economist Frédéric Bastiat wrote in *Les Harmonies économiques* (1851) that to destroy competition "is to kill intelligence." Competition is opposed to arbitrariness, privileges, and unjustified rents. It embodies "the democratic law in essence," and is perceived as a source of progress, productivity gains, and low prices.

For others, competition is a selection process in which not everyone plays on equal terms. The triumphant are not necessarily the most deserving, but rather the richest or the least scrupulous. Competition then inevitably leads to the lasting and unjustified domination of a few, to the detriment of consumers and workers. As libertarian and anarchist thinker Pierre-Joseph Proudhon wrote, "competition kills competition" and "competition, in its results, is unjust" [*System of Economic Contradictions; or, the Philosophy of Misery* (1846)].

In fact, there is some truth in both of these opposing views. On the one hand, we can think of the beneficial effects of the entry of new firms on quality, prices, and innovation. On the other hand, we can think of unfair practices, such as dumping, or anti-competitive practices, such as cartels, which artificially freeze the market to the detriment of consumers and welfare.

These two opposing views, however, are not based on any explicit analytical framework that enables one to test their relevance. Depending on the behavior of firms or the specific characteristics of the market, competition may be more or less beneficial to society, as economic analysis shows.

This book begins from a rather intuitive and widespread viewpoint that equates competition with the number of firms: the more firms there are in a market, the more intense the competition. We will show that this intuition is found in the famous "pure and perfect competition" model, which constitutes a reference for understanding competition. Indeed, with this model in mind, we can analyze different market structures, characterized by a small number of firms – monopoly and oligopoly. The main result of this approach is that when the number of firms in the market increases, competition becomes more intense and approaches the ideal situation of pure and perfect competition, characterized by the absence of market power and profits.

The second chapter shows that this initial theoretical approach is insufficient to fully understand the concrete functioning of competition. One must take into account criteria other than the number of firms in order to assess the intensity of competition. For instance, strong competition can occur with a small number of firms. We will develop an alternative approach to competition, which emphasizes the key role of the dynamic of market shares. In such a conception, competition becomes a selection process of the most efficient firms, which may temporarily lead to monopoly positions. Competition and monopoly are no longer opposites but complements.

Following the presentation of these two main theoretical approaches, the third chapter reviews the various effects of competition, as observed in practice by economists. The methodology consists of comparing the situation of a market before and after a "competitive shock," which can be of a very diverse nature: the launch of a new economic model, a patent expiry, the growth of imports from an emerging country, the opening of a sector to competition. We will analyze the impacts of increased competition on supply and demand, adopting both a microeconomic and macroeconomic perspective.

In particular, we will show that, beyond its usual effects on prices, competition can be an important factor in productivity gains and innovation.

While the dynamic of competition is mainly based on the entry of new firms, certain obstacles, both technological and behavioral, can limit its intensity. We will see in Chapter 4 that the presence of economies of scale or network effects can lead to lasting situations of oligopoly or "natural" monopoly. Moreover, even when many firms are in a market, it is not certain that consumers will take advantage of the situation, because their mobility is hampered by search costs and behavioral biases. Finally, competition within the market may be limited by the strategic behavior of incumbents, which may engage in cartels or foreclose equally efficient competitors.

The intensity of competition within a market does not only depend on the characteristics and strategies of firms; it is also influenced by policy choices. In other words, competition is always more or less regulated by public authorities, sometimes directly – think of the numerus clausus or customs duties – or indirectly, through regulations that impact the entry. In an extreme case, the state can even confer on a single firm the right to produce, which is called a "legal monopoly." On the other hand, the state can authorize any firm to operate in the market, as long as it respects the minimum quality and safety rules. In order to increase the intensity of competition, public authorities have multiple levers at their disposal. We will show in Chapter 5 that policies to open up markets to competition often meet with strong internal resistance, and are difficult to implement. The temptation for policy-makers to restrict competition – through protectionist policies, for example – is therefore great. However, we will see that in network industries, a profound movement to open up markets to competition has been underway in Europe since the 1990s.

As markets open up, government also steps in as a market "watchdog" through its competition policy, as we will demonstrate in Chapter 6. Its role, which is now central in most developed countries, is to prevent, detect, and sanction anti-competitive practices.

Chapter 1

Competition and the Primacy of the Number of Firms

The most intuitive view of competition is to equate it with the number of firms: the more firms there are in a market, the more intense the competition. This is the starting point of the famous "pure and perfect competition" model, which holds that in a competitive market, there are so many firms that none of them has market power.

Conversely, when a firm is in a monopoly position, it enjoys market power, leading to high prices and high profits. This monopoly behavior is harmful to both consumers and welfare.[1]

Between these two polar cases, we find markets characterized by a small number of firms: oligopolies. We will study the Cournot oligopoly, which is the perfect synthesis of the approach based on the

---

1   The concept of welfare is defined on page 5.

number of firms: when the number of firms increases, competition becomes more intense, and the market tends to a situation of pure and perfect competition.

I. The Canonical Model of Pure and Perfect Competition

Born out of the neoclassical school at the end of the 19th century, the model of pure and perfect competition is the starting point for understanding what a competitive market is: competition is fundamentally associated with the idea of a large number of firms.

After establishing the conditions on which this model is based, we will highlight the two main conclusions that it reaches:

- There are no long-term profits for firms.

- Pure and perfect competition is the best situation for society as a whole (consumers and producers), because consumer surplus and welfare are at a maximum.

The model of pure and perfect competition is based on several assumptions. The "purity" of competition includes three conditions:

- *Free entry and exit.* There are no legal or economic obstacles or delays to new firms' entry into or exit from the market. In particular, a firm that exits the market does not incur any *sunk cost*; it can, for example, resell its assets on the second-hand market without incurring any losses.

- *Product homogeneity.* Producers offer goods that are absolutely identical for consumer use. The price is the only variable to distinguish one product from another. For example, wheat is such a commodity.

– *Market atomicity.* The numbers of sellers and buyers are very high.

The "perfection" of competition implies transparency of information. All market participants have the same information, which is available immediately and without cost. There are no information asymmetries, with some firms being better informed than others.

Let's revisit the condition of atomicity. *Atomicity* means that each individual supplier is so small that it has no influence over the market; a firm's decision to produce more or less has no impact on the overall quantity, and therefore no impact on the price. Each supplier is a *price taker*, with the price being an external fact. To make an analogy, a firm in pure and perfect competition is like a voter in a large democracy: one individual's vote has no influence on the final result, insofar as it represents an infinitesimal part of the electorate.

Since each supplier has no impact on price, the demand function it faces is infinitely price elastic[2] – it is a horizontal line. If a firm increases its price above the market price, it loses all of its consumers when they switch to another firm that has maintained the market price. In Graph 1, we see that for a market price (which corresponds to the intersection of demand and supply) of €5, the quantity offered by a particular firm has no influence on the price – the demand is a horizontal line. If the firm wants to sell at €5.10, it will not sell anything; the demand for this price is nil.

---

2   The price elasticity of demand measures the change in demand for a product (in percentage) after a price change (in percentage). It ranges from 0 to -∞. If the price elasticity of demand is high (in absolute terms), this means that a rise in price implies a very large fall in demand. If it is zero, it means that demand does not change after a price increase.

Graph 1. Firm's demand and market equilibrium

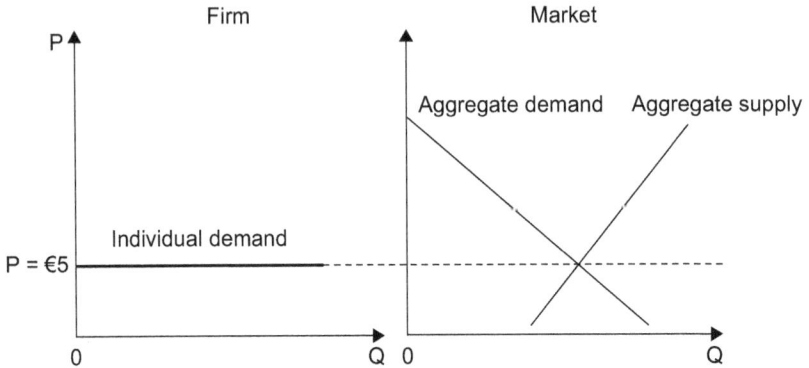

From these different conditions, we obtain a first important result: in a market with pure and perfect competition, firms will not make any profit in the long run. Recall that the profit (Π) is defined as the multiplication of the margin – the difference between the price (P) and the marginal cost of production (c) – by the quantities (Q):

$$\pi = \underbrace{(P - c)}_{\text{margin}} \times Q$$

Recall also that the marginal cost is the cost of producing an additional unit. Marginal cost includes the cost of purchasing raw materials, workers' wages, and any relevant cost component that varies with the production level. In the absence of fixed costs, the marginal cost is equal to the average unit cost. In the following discussion, we will assume for simplicity that there is no fixed cost and that the marginal cost is constant and therefore represented by a horizontal line (each additional unit always costs the same to produce).

If the price is higher than the marginal cost, firms will make a short-term profit. But this situation will only be temporary. Indeed, in

4

a situation of pure and perfect competition where there are no barriers to entry, new firms will enter the market, which will cause the market price to fall until profits become nil.

Another way of presenting this first result is to say that in a situation of pure and perfect competition, firms have no long-term market power, i.e., no capability to maintain their prices above their unit cost. Market power is measured by the Lerner index, defined as the ratio between the margin (i.e., the difference between the price and the marginal cost) and the price:[3]

$$\text{Lerner index} = (P - c) / P$$

In a situation of pure and perfect competition, this index is equal to zero, since the price (P) is equal to the marginal cost (c).

A second important result of the pure and perfect competition model is that it maximizes welfare.

Let's start by defining welfare (W). *Welfare* represents the total gain to society resulting from the exchange between consumers and producers. It includes consumer surplus (SC) and the profits (Π) that each firm (i) makes:

$$W\,(P) = SC\,(P) + \sum_{i=1}^{n} \Pi_i\,(P) \text{ with } i = 1, \ldots n$$

Consumer surplus is the difference between consumers' maximum willingness to pay and the price paid.

To measure the total consumer surplus, we can start with a demand function, which expresses the quantity demanded (Q), as a function of the price (P). For simplicity, we will take a linear demand function:

$$P = a - bQ \text{ with } a > \text{marginal cost } c \text{ and } a, b > 0$$

---

3   An equivalent ratio is: $1 - (\text{profits} / \text{value added})$. In competition, since profits are zero, this ratio equals 1.

In a situation of pure and perfect competition, all consumers pay the same price (Pppc), which is equal to the marginal cost (c). The consumers' total surplus, represented by the shaded area in Graph 2, is equal to the difference between each consumer's maximum willingness to pay (represented by the demand function) and the price paid (P_{ppc}) multiplied by the quantity (Q_{ppc}).

Firms make no profit since they sell at their marginal cost. The total welfare is therefore equal to the consumer surplus.

Graph 2. Pure and perfect competition and welfare

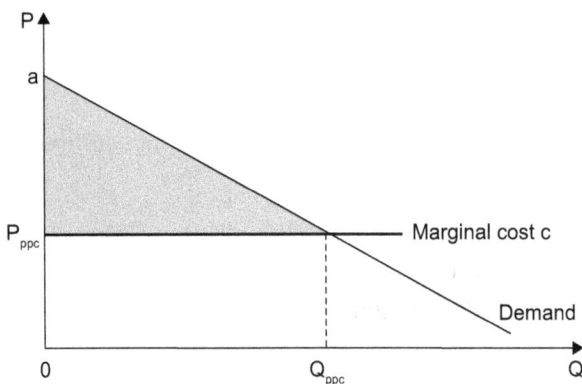

A situation of pure and perfect competition produces maximal welfare. Indeed, if the price were below marginal cost, firms would suffer losses. These losses would be greater than the increase in consumer surplus, resulting in lower total welfare. Conversely, if the price were higher than the marginal cost, firms would make a profit; but the profit would be less than the drop in consumer surplus, resulting in a lowered total welfare.

II. Alone in the Market: the Monopoly

In contrast to pure and perfect competition, a *monopoly* is a market structure characterized by the presence of a single firm that is not threatened (at least in the short term) by the entry of competitors. Unlike pure and perfect competition, a monopoly can set a price above its marginal cost without fearing that consumers will switch to other suppliers. A monopoly enjoys market power, but with limits (1). Compared to pure and perfect competition, a monopoly leads to a decrease in total welfare. It is also a source of several inefficiencies (2). In this sense, a monopoly constitutes a market structure opposed to that of pure and perfect competition.

1. Monopoly Is Malthusian

Insofar as it is alone in the market, a monopoly is not constrained by any competitors. It therefore enjoys the power to set its price; a monopoly is a *price maker.* The only constraint a monopoly faces is the willingness to pay of consumers, who may be more or less sensitive to price.

To understand how a monopoly sets its price, we can use an intuitive approach. Suppose there is a firm alone in the market with a constant marginal cost (c). It faces a decreasing demand: when the price falls, the number of consumers rises.

What price will it set? If it sets a very high price, it will have few consumers but will make a large margin on each of them. If it lowers its price, two opposite effects will confront the firm:

- It will gain new consumers, increasing its total revenue (quantity effect).

- It will lose margin on previous consumers, reducing its total revenue (margin loss effect).

The more the monopoly lowers its price, the more consumers it has, but the greater the negative effect on the margin will be compared to the increase in quantities. Its marginal revenue, defined as the variation in total revenue, will decrease. The monopoly will therefore stop lowering its price when the marginal revenue is equal to the cost of serving one more customer (the marginal cost). Graphically, the monopoly sets its price and quantity when the marginal cost intersects the marginal revenue (Graph 3).

We can see in Graph 3 that the monopoly sets a higher price P^M than in a situation of pure and perfect competition. As a consequence, the monopoly offers a smaller quantity Q^M; we call the monopoly's action *Malthusian* behavior.[4] Since the price is higher than the marginal cost, the monopoly makes a profit, which is equal to the shaded rectangle.

Graph 3. The monopoly equilibrium

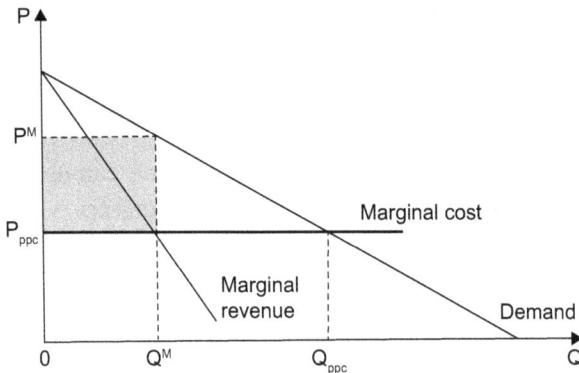

The monopoly enjoys market power; it can raise its price above marginal cost without fearing the loss of all its consumers. The extent of its market power depends on factors such as the price elasticity of demand.

---

4   Malthusian behavior refers to the act of restricting quantities. It comes from the doctrine developed by economist Thomas Malthus, who advocated a restriction of the birth rate in demographic matters.

Indeed, if consumers are not very price sensitive, the monopoly can raise its price sharply. Conversely, if demand is price elastic, the monopoly has little market power. It can be shown that the market power of a monopoly depends inversely on the price elasticity of demand (ε) in absolute value:

$$\text{Market power of a monopoly} = 1/\varepsilon$$

Let's take a pharmaceutical firm selling a staple drug facing a demand that is not very elastic. If it is in a monopoly situation, it will set a high selling price compared to its marginal cost. For example, the U.S. Senate Committee on Aging observed in a 2016 report that there had been sharp price increases on certain drugs, even though their patents had fallen into the public domain. These were drugs for which, given the small size of the market (few patients were concerned), there was no generic competition. Another example is the production site of Cuprimine, which treats Wilson's disease. A "speculator" bought it in 2010 and decided to increase the drug's price from $93 to $26,188.64 – an increase of . . . 5,786%. This increase is the consequence of the low price elasticity of demand, as patients have no choice but to buy this treatment.

Having looked at the case of a monopoly on the supply side, we can apply similar reasoning on the demand side to a *monopsony*. Since it is the only buyer, a monopsony will exert its market power by driving prices down. For example, in the labor market, a monopsony situation arises when there is only one employer in a local area and the workers are not mobile. In this situation, the monopsony can lower the wage without fearing that workers will go elsewhere.[5] The subject of the monopsony is an old one in economics. The 19th century frequently saw large steel or textile firms being the sole purchasers of labor within local employment areas. This situation leads to

---

5   To fight against this market power, employees can opt to join together and form a union. Hicks (1935) defined the union as an organization aimed at counterbalancing the monopsony power of the employer.

downward pressure on wages. Monopsony situations in the labor market have not disappeared in today's world (see OECD [2019b]). In particular, as we will see in Chapter 2, industrial concentration has increased considerably in many markets, especially under the influence of digital technologies. In some U.S. employment areas, a few firms are the employers. This employer concentration in a given geographical area leads to lower wages (see Azar et al. [2017]; Benmelech et al. [2018]).

2. The Monopoly's Trial

When we compare the monopoly situation with that of pure and perfect competition, we see that a monopoly has a double effect on total welfare:

- *It takes over a part of the consumer surplus* (area B). Some consumers continue to buy the product, despite its higher price. This transfer of surplus corresponds to the total profit made by the monopoly (Graph 4).

- *It reduces total welfare* (*deadweight loss*). The monopoly's profit is lower than the decrease in consumer surplus. In fact, in a competitive situation, consumer surplus is equal to the area (A + B + D); in a monopoly situation, consumer surplus is represented by area A. Consumers have therefore lost (B + D), while the monopoly has made a profit equal to area B – the loss of surplus is equivalent to triangle D. This is because the price increase has led some consumers to give up buying the product. In 1954, Harberger measured the value of this deadweight loss in the case of the United States and concluded that it was low at the macroeconomic level – less than 0.1% of the gross national product (GNP).

Compared to a pure and perfect competitive market, a monopoly market is undesirable for society as a whole, as it reduces total welfare. This is referred to as the *allocative inefficiency* of a monopoly.

Graph 4. Monopoly and welfare

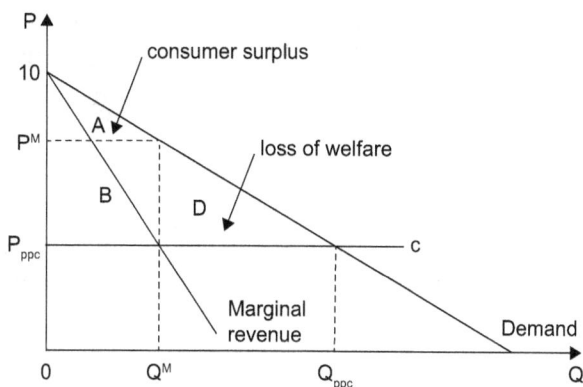

Beyond this allocative inefficiency, a monopoly can also generate three other distortions.

First, a monopoly has less incentive to control its costs than a firm in a competitive situation. This inefficiency is called *X-inefficiency* or productive inefficiency. It can be summed up by John Hicks's famous quote (1935): "*The best of all monopoly profits is a quiet life.*" A monopoly knows that if its costs increase, it will pass on part of this cost increase to its selling price, without fearing the loss of all its consumers. In a pure and perfect competitive market, this situation is impossible: an increase in a firm's marginal cost mechanically increases its price (since profits are zero), resulting in the loss of all its consumers.

Secondly, to the extent that a monopoly already benefits from a rent, it has a low incentive to innovate : this phenomenon is known as "the laurel effect" (Arrow 1962). The monopoly causes a *dynamic inefficiency*. Let's take as an example a firm in a monopoly situation

11

with a drug: this monopoly makes a profit of €50. If tomorrow it discovers a therapeutic vaccine that replaces its drug, its profit will increase to €80. The monopoly's incentive to discover the vaccine is therefore equal to (€80 − €50), or €30. The monopoly takes into account the fact that by innovating, it replaces itself by cannibalizing the sales of its drug. Conversely, a firm in a situation of pure and perfect competition has a strong incentive to discover the vaccine. The incentive is equal to (€50 €0) because the firm makes no profit before the discovery. However, if the monopoly is threatened by the entry of a competitor, then its incentive to innovate becomes stronger than that of the entrant. Indeed, suppose the monopoly profit is €50 and the entry of a new firm will decrease the total profit from €50 to €30 (each firm will make a profit of €15). The entrant's incentive to enter the market is therefore €15, while the monopoly's incentive to stay in a monopoly position is (€50 − €15), or €35. To avoid losing its position, the monopoly is willing to spend much more than the entrant.

Finally, when the monopoly comes from a legal restriction, firms will try to obtain this rent by spending money, as shown by the theory of *rent-seeking*. This spending can take many forms, both illegal (such as bribes) and legal (such as subsidies to a political party). If firms compete to become a legal monopoly, the total expenditure will be equal to... the monopoly profit. In Graph 4, area B, which is equal to the profit of the firm that obtained the legal monopoly, has been lost by all other firms. Initiated in the 1970s, the first empirical studies on rent-seeking in developing countries concluded that the waste due to rent-seeking behavior amounted to more than 7% of GNP in India and 15% in Turkey (see Krueger, 1974).

This highly critical view on the monopoly and its inefficiencies must be discussed.

First, pure monopoly situations are quite rare in practice. Even in cases where a firm is granted a legal monopoly, such as the SNCF for high-speed trains in France until 2020, there is often intermodal competition (e.g., between trains and planes). The notion of monopoly therefore depends on the contours of the relevant market.

Second, as we shall see in Chapters 3 and 4, we have not thus far considered the origins of monopoly. A monopoly is economically unjustified if it results from arbitrary behavior by the state or abusive behavior, without any counterpart in terms of efficiency gains. But conversely:

– There are situations known as *natural monopolies* in which there is only one firm, given the magnitude of fixed costs.

– Monopoly can result from the intrinsic superiority of a firm over its competitors. For example, an innovative firm will benefit, through a patent, from a legitimate but temporary rent. The patent leads to a high price for a certain time, but it encourages firms to innovate.

– Monopoly can also be a prerequisite for innovation, as Joseph Schumpeter pointed out. Indeed, innovation is costly and difficult to finance externally, given the risk of failing to discover. The advantage of a monopoly is that it already makes profit and can invest internally in R&D. On the other hand, it will be difficult for a firm in a pure and perfect competitive market to innovate, because it will not have access to external financial resources.

III. Between Monopoly and Competition: Oligopoly

Between the two polar market structures of pure and perfect competition and monopoly, we find imperfect market structures, characterized by a small number of firms: duopoly, when there are two firms, and oligopoly beyond that. Oligopoly situations are numerous. We can cite, for example, the duopoly between Airbus and Boeing for the production of large airliners, or the subscription video on demand (SVOD) market, in which many firms operate, such as Netflix, Disney+, and Amazon Prime Video.

The analysis of an oligopoly market is complex, because each firm exerts influence on other firms. This interdependence does not exist in a pure and perfect competitive market, given the large number of firms.[6] There, no firm has the power to influence the behavior of other firms. The same is true for a monopoly, since there are no competitors. The study of oligopoly therefore requires the analysis of the reciprocal interactions between several firms.

Numerous models of oligopoly exist. In particular, we can distinguish between the Bertrand duopoly, the Stackelberg duopoly, the Hotelling duopoly, and the Cournot duopoly. Each model is based on specific hypotheses – particularly the decision variable and simultaneity (Table 1).

Table 1. The different types of duopoly/oligopoly

	Decision variable: price	Decision variable: quantities	Decision variable: location
Simultaneous decision (both firms decide at the same time)	Bertrand duopoly	Cournot duopoly	Hotelling duopoly
Sequential decision (one firm decides before the other)	Price leadership	Stackelberg duopoly	

Among these different models, the one that Augustin Cournot (1838) developed is particularly interesting and often used in empirical studies.

---

6   In this respect, we can see the paradoxical nature of pure and perfect competition: each firm is fairly passive and has no real strategy for attracting consumers, insofar as it is a price taker.

1. Cournot's Duopoly

Let's start with the case of two firms competing in a market. We will assume they have the same unit cost and produce the same goods. They must decide at the same time on their levels of production (and, therefore, on the price they will charge).

In this duopoly situation, we can demonstrate that the total quantity produced is higher than the monopoly quantity but lower than the pure and perfect competition quantity: the Cournot duopoly is an intermediate market structure (Figure 5).[7] We can deduce that the Cournot duopoly price is higher than the price in a pure and perfect competitive market, but lower than the monopoly price.

Graph 5. The duopoly as an intermediate market

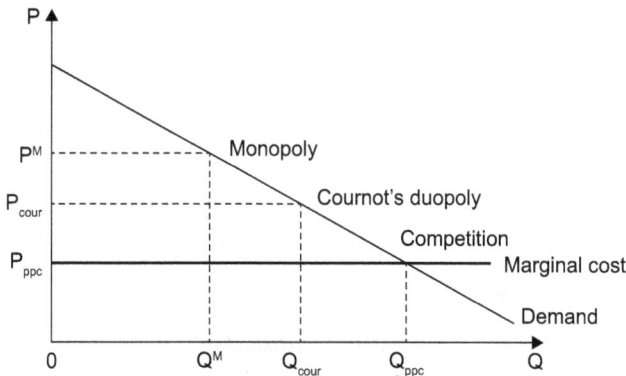

Profits in a duopoly situation are lower than those of a monopoly; two firms cannot collectively obtain a profit as high as a single firm. This very important result can be explained intuitively. Imagine a firm A, which is alone in the market (Figure 1). Since there is no

---

7   With a linear demand function, we can show that the total Cournot quantity is two thirds of the pure and perfect competition quantity.

competitive pressure, it achieves a monopoly profit of €100. But if firm B enters the market, firm B will exert downward pressure on the price, which will reduce the total profit to €66. After the entry of firm B, the total profit cannot remain as high as it was in a monopoly situation. Moreover, as two firms are now in the market, they will share the remaining total profit (equal to €66).

The result is a sharp drop in profit for firm A, resulting from both the competition effect (€34 less) and the sharing of the remaining profits (€33 less). After the entry of firm B, firm A's profits have therefore fallen from €100 to €33 (a fall of €67).

Figure 1. From monopoly to Cournot's duopoly

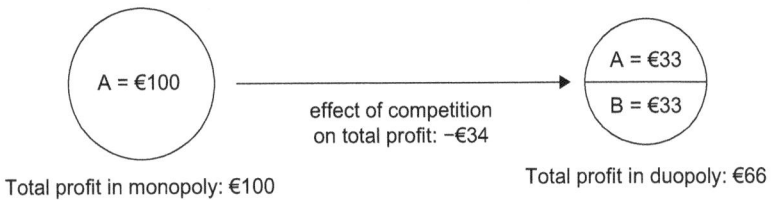

A = €100

effect of competition
on total profit: −€34

A = €33

B = €33

Total profit in monopoly: €100

Total profit in duopoly: €66

Different variants of Cournot's duopoly can be developed:

- *The two firms have different costs.* In this case, the firm with the lower cost will produce more and obtain higher profits than its competitor.

- *The two firms offer differentiated products.* The intensity of competition will be attenuated because their products are not perfectly substitutable for consumers. It can be shown that the more the products are differentiated, the more the profits of each firm increase, approaching the monopoly profit.

- *One of the two firms – called the* leader *– chooses its production level before the other.* The leader will make a higher profit.

Indeed, it takes advantage of being the first to produce more than in the Cournot duopoly. The *follower* firm, on the other hand, will set a lower level of production, compared to a simultaneous situation. This leader-follower model is often referred to as the Stackelberg duopoly.

2. From Duopoly to Cournot's Oligopoly

Cournot's model can be scaled to include more than two firms. In this case, it can be shown that as the number of firms increases, the market progressively approaches pure and perfect competition: the total quantity increases; the price progressively decreases towards the marginal cost (Graph 6); the profit of each firm tends towards zero; and the total welfare increases and approaches that obtained in a pure and perfect competitive situation.

In a Cournot oligopoly, therefore, the number of firms in the market plays a decisive role: the greater the number of firms, the closer the market is to a perfectly competitive market.

Graph 6. Evolution of the price according to the number of firms

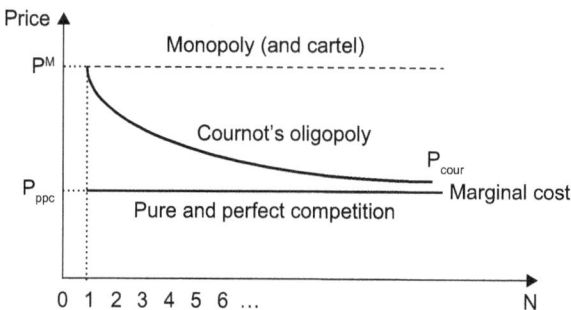

Note: A multi-firm monopoly is a cartel (see Chapter 4). A situation of pure and perfect competition with a single firm is possible in a contestable market (see Chapter 2).

Cournot's oligopoly is very useful for understanding empirically how a market evolves when the number of firms varies. Two examples can illustrate this.

First, if a firm merges with its competitor, we can expect an increase in price and profits. Let's take two firms A and B competing in a Cournot duopoly and making a total profit of €66. Firm A decides to buy firm B; it then becomes a monopoly. Firm A will make a double gain from the merger:

– It will recover the €33 of firm B's profits;

– Now in a monopoly position, it can increase its price and thus its profits by €34. Its total profit has therefore risen from €33 to €100 (Figure 2), a positive variation of €67.

Figure 2. The effect of a merger in Cournot's duopoly

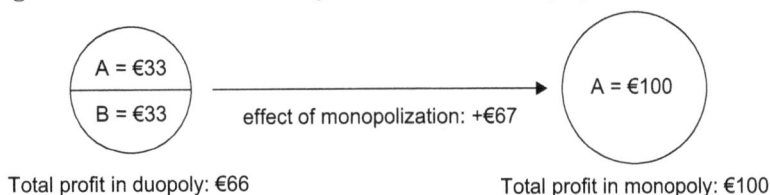

A = €33
B = €33   effect of monopolization: +€67   A = €100

Total profit in duopoly: €66   Total profit in monopoly: €100

For example, in 2013, the European Commission blocked Ryanair's takeover project of Irish airline Aer Lingus because the merger would have led to a monopoly of the 46 air routes over which the two airlines were competing. After the merger, the new firm would have behaved like a monopoly and raised airfares.

Second, the entry of a new firm will lead to increased competition, which will lower the price and increase the total welfare. For example, suppose that firms A and B are competing à la Cournot, and each firm is making a €33 profit. A new firm, firm C, with the same production cost, enters the market. The entry of firm C will lower the price and profits. The total profit is no longer €66 but €42, i.e., €14 per firm. The change from two to three firms has a double negative effect on firms A and B:

- As the total profit has decreased by €24, their profits have each decreased by €12.

- The remaining profit must be divided between three and not two. Instead of earning €21 each (i.e., half of €42), firms A and B each make €14.

They have lost (€12 + €7), or €19. Their individual profit has fallen from €33 to €14 (Figure 3).

Figure 3. The effect of entering Cournot's duopoly

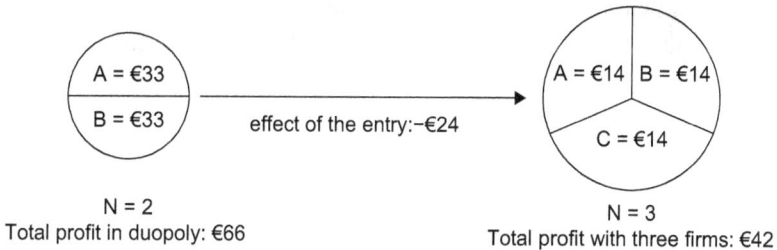

The impact of a new firm entry can be illustrated by the case of Free Mobile, which entered the French mobile phone market in 2012. The number of firms increased from three to four. A simulation of the entry was carried out by the French Treasury Department (2009) based on the Cournot oligopoly model. The study concluded that Free Mobile's entry would lead to a 7% drop in prices, resulting in a reduction in total profits of €852 million per year for the three operators. In return for this decrease in profits, consumer surplus would increase by €1,224 million per year, resulting in an increase in total welfare of €373 million per year.[8]

---

8   In retrospect, the entry of Free Mobile in 2012 led to a greater price decrease than that predicted in the model, of around 25% over two years. See Chapter 3.

At the end of this chapter, we have a first vision of competition, derived from the model of pure and perfect competition:

- By its characteristics, competition is a market structure with a very large number of firms; as such, it is opposed to a monopoly situation. If we look at it step by step, the intensity of competition increases with the number of firms, as shown by Cournot's oligopoly.

- By its consequences, competition is a situation in which firms have no market power and therefore make no profit. In a situation of pure and perfect competition, the market power is nil. Competition is the opposite of the case of a monopoly, which enjoys strong market power. Cournot's oligopoly appears as an intermediate situation in terms of profits: as the number of firms increases, market power decreases.

Chapter 2

Competition, Beyond the Number of Firms

The previous chapter demonstrated that the number of firms in the market plays a central role in explaining competition: the higher the number, the stronger the competition – the extreme case being a market of pure and perfect competition.

However, the criterion of the number of firms is neither necessary nor sufficient to assess the intensity of competition. Other market characteristics must be taken into account – in particular, the distribution of market shares between firms. Moreover, it is not always necessary to have a large number of firms to achieve a pure and perfect competitive market; strong competition is possible with just two firms in the market, or even only one.

Beyond the number of firms and the market characteristics, we can also question the idea that competition is necessarily opposed to monopoly. In reality, if we adopt a dynamic vision, monopoly appears to be the temporary and natural consequence of a competitive process leading to selecting the most efficient firms. This dynamic vision of competition invites us to rethink how we analyze market concentration, which is no longer necessarily a sign of a lack of competition. In this respect, an important debate has been taking place in the United States in order to better understand the causes and effects of market concentration observed since the beginning of the 21st century. The question on the table? Is high concentration a sign of weakening of competition or not?

I. The Intensity of Competition Depends on Multiple Factors

To assess the competitive intensity of a market, it is not enough to count the number of firms; the specific market characteristics must also be considered (1). Moreover, the number of firms is not always relevant. A firm may be alone in the market and in a competitive situation (2).

1. Structural Characteristics of the Market

When comparing two markets with the same number of firms, the intensity of competition, as measured by the Lerner index, will not necessarily be the same if the structural characteristics of the two markets differ. Without claiming to be exhaustive, we can identify several factors that influence the intensity of competition (Figure 4).

Figure 4. The main factors affecting market power

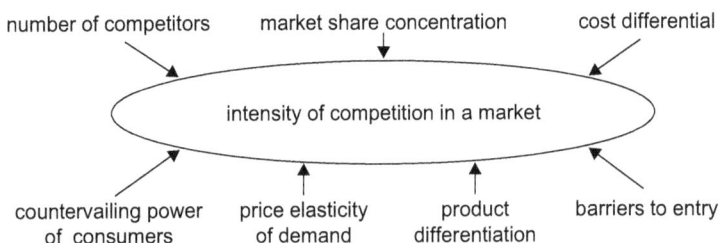

number of competitors   market share concentration   cost differential

intensity of competition in a market

countervailing power of consumers   price elasticity of demand   product differentiation   barriers to entry

The first factor is *market share concentration*. The more asymmetric the distribution of market shares between firms, the more likely competition in the market will be weak. To measure concentration, we can calculate the market share of the leaders. This is called the *concentration ratio* (CR). For example, if the CR_4 is equal to 80%, it means that the four biggest firms represent 80% of the market.

We can also calculate the Herfindahl-Hirschman Index (HHI), which is defined as the sum of the squared market shares of each firm:

$$HHI = \sum_{i=1}^{n} s_i^2 \; x \; 100 \text{ with } s_i \in [0, 100] \text{ and } i = 1, 2, \dots, N.$$

This index is worth 10,000 in the case of a monopoly (100^2) and tends towards 0 when the number of firms tends towards infinity, with symmetric market shares. The value of the index depends both on the total number of firms (N) and on the distribution of their market shares; for a given number of firms, the index is high when the distribution of market shares is unequal.

For instance, if the market includes four firms of identical size, $N = 4$ and the market share of each firm is 25%, the value of the Herfindahl-Hirschman Index will be: $4 \times 25^2 = 2{,}500$. If, however, the market consists of four firms but the market shares are 70%, 10%, 10%, and 10%, the value of the HHI will be higher: $70^2 + 3 \times 10^2 = 5{,}200$.

In a Cournot model with N firms, the market power (measured by the markup) increases with the value of the HHI, for a given level of the price elasticity of demand ($\mathcal{E}$):

$$\text{Margin rate in Cournot} = \frac{HHI}{\mathcal{E}}$$

This means that the more concentrated a market, the higher the margins. The intensity of competition is therefore lower in a concentrated market.

A second factor to consider is the cost differential between firms. In a Cournot duopoly, the market will be more competitive if one of the two firms has a lower production cost. For example, if we compare a market containing two *high-cost* firms with a market that has one *high-cost* and one *low-cost* firm, competition will be stronger in the second case.

A third factor is the degree of product differentiation. Many models of differentiation have been developed (monopolistic competition, vertical differentiation, etc.). Each model concludes that strong product differentiation reduces the competition intensity. In an extreme case, if two firms produce completely different products, each firm is in a monopoly situation in regard to its own demand. Markets with differentiated products are very common in consumer goods, where brands play an important role in consumer choice. For example, in the luxury car market, there are a large number of firms, but car brands are very different (e.g., a Ferrari is not identical to a Porsche).

A fourth factor relates to the entry barriers. When barriers are high, it is unlikely that a new competitor will enter. Therefore, incumbent firms can raise prices above marginal cost. Barriers to entry can have different origins, such as legal barriers or economies of scale.

A fifth factor is the price elasticity of demand, as we have already seen in the case of a monopoly. If consumers are very price sensitive, the firms' market power is low and price approaches marginal cost.

The final factor concerns the countervailing power of clients. A reduction in the number of firms in the market does not necessarily increase prices if clients have strong bargaining power. This argument is often invoked by suppliers that sell their products via supermarkets and decide to merge: as supermarkets possess a scarce resource (access to the shelf), and as there are few central purchasing agencies, they can exert downward pressure on prices. Moreover, as supermarkets often develop their own private labels, they enjoy bargaining power pertaining to entry-level products, threatening suppliers with delisting.

This increasing complexity in the analysis of competition has led some authors to establish a causal link between the characteristics of a market and the intensity of competition.

The structuralist school (also called the Harvard School – see, for example, Bain [1956]) thus developed in the 1960s the famous SCP (structure–conduct–performance) paradigm:

- Market structures (S) are characterized by the number of firms, the concentration of market shares, the degree of product differentiation, and the height of entry barriers. When the number of firms is low, the market is concentrated, the products are differentiated, and the entry barriers are high, the market will be close to a monopoly. Conversely, if the market is atomized and the market shares are not concentrated, and if the products are homogeneous and the entry is free, the market structure will be similar to pure and perfect competition.

- Conduct (C) refers mainly to firms' pricing and investment strategies. Behavior depends directly on the market structures.

- Performance (P) expresses the firms' market power and is measured by the markup or the Lerner index. The performance indicator can be interpreted in terms of competitive intensity: a high level of market power means that competitive intensity is low.

According to the structuralist school, the characteristics of market structures (S) determine the conduct of firms (C), which explains their performances (P).

Figure 5. The SCP paradigm

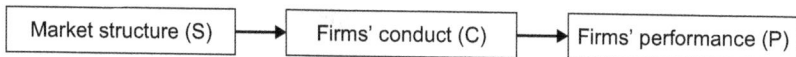

25

For example, in a highly concentrated market protected by entry barriers (S), firms will engage in tacit or explicit collusive behavior (C), which will result in high profits (P). Similarly, in a concentrated market with a dominant firm, the dominant firm will try to exclude competitors by, for example, charging predatory prices, which will result in high profits (P).

According to the SCP approach, public authorities (through competition policy) must intervene at two points, in order to maintain competition:

- On market structures (S); for example, by limiting mergers;

- On conduct (C), by putting large firms under surveillance, in order to prevent anti-competitive strategies such as collusion or abuse of dominance.

2. Competition – with a Small Number of Firms

So far, we have assumed that the number of firms plays a key role in competitive intensity, even though other factors should be considered. But we can also say that the number of firms is not necessarily useful in assessing the intensity of competition. Strong competition can exist with few firms in the market.

Let's start with the case of a duopoly. Two firms must choose their prices simultaneously, without any capacity constraint (unlike the Cournot model described in Chapter 1). This is the case of the Bertrand duopoly (1883).

Consider two firms A and B. They produce an identical good with the same production cost (c), and they must set their prices at the same time. If one of the two firms sets a higher price than its competitor, it loses all its consumers, since the only choice criterion for consumers is the price. Based on this principle, each firm will set a price equal to the marginal cost:

$$PA = PB = c$$

This famous result, known as Bertrand's paradox, shows that the intensity of competition in a market does not depend on the number of firms but on the nature of the competition: price competition between only two firms without capacity constraints leads to a result similar to that of pure and perfect competition.

This theoretical result corresponds fairly well to that observed in a bidding market. For example, let's imagine a bid for the construction of a school; the production cost is estimated at €2 million. Each firm has to post a price without knowing the price of its competitor. If a firm bids €2.2 million, for example, it runs the risk of losing the bid. Each firm is afraid that its competitor will bid slightly less than its own, so they each decide to bid €2 million.

We can go further in challenging the atomicity hypothesis by showing that the result of pure and perfect competition can be achieved with only one firm. This is the case of a *contestable market* (Baumol et al., 1982).

A market is considered to be contestable when three conditions are met:

- New firms and incumbent firms have access to the same production technologies.

- Entry costs can be recovered if the new firm exits the market, i.e., there are no *sunk costs*. For example, if a firm enters the airline sector, it must bear the fixed cost of purchasing an aircraft; however, this cost is not sunk insofar as the firm can resell its aircraft on the second-hand market.

– The entry time is shorter than the time required for incumbent firms to change their prices.

In a contestable market, if a single firm is threatened by the entry of new competitors, it has no choice but to charge a price equal to marginal cost. Indeed, if it charges a price above the competitive price, a new supplier will immediately enter the market, offering a slightly lower price, therefore "taking the place" of the incumbent firm. In a contestable market, a single firm has no market power. With such an approach, what matters in assessing the intensity of competition is not the number of firms actually present in the market but the threat of entry.

The theory of contestable markets is a *standard ideal*, which is rarely found in its pure form in the real economic world. However, some markets with relatively low barriers to entry and exit are close to a contestable market. This is the case for air transport, which has given rise to empirical studies on the role of potential competition in determining the price of air tickets. Morrison (2001) studied the impact that the entry of low-cost airline Southwest Airlines had on ticket prices of competing U.S. airlines. He showed that the downward impact on the price is not limited to the routes directly competing with Southwest Airlines; it also spreads to the entire airline market through what is known as the *Southwest effect*: even when Southwest Airlines is not present on a route between two points A and B, the incumbent operators lower their prices in order to prevent any future entry. This occurs when Southwest is already present on other routes from airports A and B; its presence alone induces competitors to preemptively lower prices by 33% (Table 2). When Southwest is present at substitutable departure or arrival airports but not on the same route, competitors preemptively lower prices by 13.1%. This effect is in line with the theory of contestable markets: the mere possibility of a new firm entry forces the incumbents to adjust their prices downwards in advance.

Table 2. Fare response of incumbent airlines to Southwest's entry

Category	Variable	Coefficient	Standard Error	Effect on Fares*
Actual Competition				
	At-At-Serves	−0.620	0.023	−46.2%
	At-Near-Serves	−0.306	0.023	−26.4%
	Near-Near-Serves	−0.167	0.029	−15.4%
Potential Competition				
	At-At-Does not Serve	−0.401	0.027	−33.0%
	At-Near-Does not Serve	−0.140	0.033	−13.1%
	Near-Near-Does not Serve	0.188	0.033	20.7%
	At-Far-Serves	−0.125	0.021	−11.8%
	Near-Far-Serves	−0.067	0.024	−6.5%

Source: Morrison (2001)

II. Competition as a Selection Process

So far, we have analyzed the market structures in a static way; the configuration of a market, either in terms of the number of firms or the market's
characteristics, has been considered an intangible fact. But a market
structure can change over time. A market with a large number of firms
can evolve into a monopoly situation and vice versa. This dynamic
approach leads to rethinking competition as a selection process (1).
Market concentration then appears as the logical and temporary consequence of competition, as illustrated by the contemporary debate in the
United States regarding the high concentration of markets (2).

1. When Competition Leads
to Temporary Monopoly

In the model of pure and perfect competition, we have seen that firms
make no profit, as they have no market power. Conversely, a monopoly
enjoys market power and makes a profit. If we adopt a static approach,
competition and monopoly are opposed.

But these two market structures should not be opposed when adopting a dynamic approach. A monopoly would then appear as the temporary consequence of competition, defined as a selection process of the most efficient firms.

To understand this approach, which was initiated in particular by Austrian economists (Hayek [1948], Schumpeter [1911, 1943]), we must go back to the original notion of *competition*. Competition is similar to a sporting activity in which each player tries to get the better of rivals. In the track world, competition is a process whereby several players compete at the start (large numbers), but only one crosses the finish line first. If we transpose this metaphor to the economy, competition becomes an ongoing process in which a large number of firms compete in the market, with one firm winning out over the others in the end because its product is considered better by consumers. Competition leads to a shift from an atomistic situation to an oligopoly or even a monopoly situation. Competition does not exclude the situation whereby a single firm may be alone in the market for a given period of time. Competition and monopoly are therefore the two inseparable sides of market dynamics.

Figure 6. Market dynamics

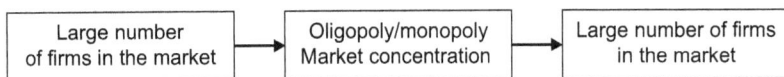

Large number of firms in the market	→	Oligopoly/monopoly Market concentration	→	Large number of firms in the market

Since competition is a dynamic process, the SCP model we saw earlier – which starts from market structures (S) to explain the performance of firms (P) – must be inverted. It is the conduct (C) and performance (P) of firms that determine industrial concentration (Figure 7). For example, if a firm launches a better product on the market, industrial concentration will increase (see McGee, 1971).

Figure 7. The SCP relationship revisited

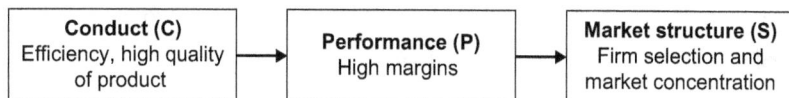

Conduct (C)	Performance (P)	Market structure (S)
Efficiency, high quality of product	→ High margins →	Firm selection and market concentration

If we consider competition to be a dynamic process that self-perpetuates, it is no longer necessary to intervene in order to reduce market concentration, contrary to what the structuralist school advocates. In this respect, the Chicago School (see Bork, 1973) considers competition policy to be, at best, useless and, at worst, harmful to competition, as it protects inefficient firms and curbs the process of *creative destruction*. Paradoxically, they believe, competition policy would turn against itself. It would no longer defend the competition process, characterized by the selection of the most efficient firms. Instead, it would maintain small and inefficient competitors in the market.

This dynamic of competition is fundamentally based on a process of innovation/imitation described as *creative destruction* (Schumpeter, 1911). Initially, a firm tries to escape price competition by launching a new product or process on the market (Figure 8), obtaining a temporary monopoly position. This incentive to innovate is strong if the firm considers it will appropriate *ex post* all the fruits of its innovative efforts. In this respect, the existence of an intellectual property system (patent, copyright, trademark) that guarantees innovators a temporary exclusive right to an innovation is important to stimulate competition.

But this monopoly situation will not last. The innovative firm will quickly be imitated, the patents will fall into the public domain, and competitors will return to the market. Prices and profits will fall before a new innovation is launched on the market.

From this perspective, the rent enjoyed by innovative firms is simply the temporary and deserved reward for their technological or commercial superiority. This rent is of a transitory nature, since market forces (through imitation) will quickly restore prices close to production costs through the entry of new firms.

Figure 8. The Schumpeterian dynamics of creative destruction

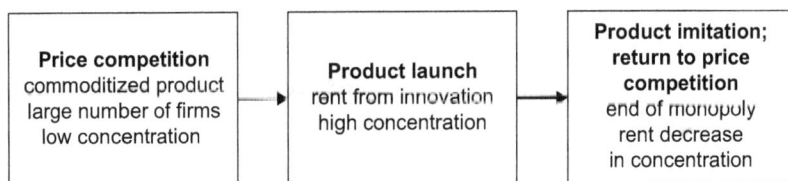

Price competition commoditized product large number of firms low concentration	**Product launch** rent from innovation high concentration	**Product imitation; return to price competition** end of monopoly rent decrease in concentration

The process of creative destruction does not only mean that new firms and products will replace older ones. It also implies that these innovations lead to productivity gains and are therefore a source of economic growth. At the macroeconomic level, we should observe a causal relationship between the dynamics of creative destruction and the growth rate, as highlighted by Aghion and Howitt (for a summary, see Aghion and Howitt, 2010).

Such an approach leads to an understanding of competition that is quite different from the understanding of the model of pure and perfect competition, as developed in Chapter 1. A market can be described as competitive if there are no obstacles to entry and exit. A competitive market is therefore a market where entry and exit are basically free.

The way of measuring the intensity of competition in a market is then modified. The concentration of market shares and the Lerner index are no longer good indicators, as they do not take into account the market dynamics. Indeed, a market can be very concentrated at a given moment simply because one firm has succeeded in differentiating itself from the others. The question is rather whether this market power will last over time; if market entry is free, market power will be transitory unless the dominant firm remains in a monopoly situation by continuing to innovate. The intensity of competition in a market is best measured by an indicator such as firms' entry and exit rate.

2. Concentration versus Competition

We have seen two rather different notions of competition, which can almost be "opposed":

- A rather pessimistic approach that considers market concentration to be the sign of a lack of competition that leads to unjustified profits.

- A more optimistic approach that concludes that market concentration is the result of the greater efficiency of some firms.

Table 3. Two approaches to competition and concentration

	Pessimistic approach	Optimistic approach
Intellectual origins	Brandeis Movement, Harvard School	Schumpeter, Hayek, Chicago School
Definition of competition	Situation characterized by a large number of firms and zero profits	Selection process for the most effective firms
Nature of the approach	Static or comparative approach	Dynamic approach
Main condition of a competitive market	• Large number of firms • Low market concentration • No barriers to entry	Freedom of entry

	Pessimistic approach	Optimistic approach
Measure of the competition's intensity	Number of competitors, market shares and market concentration (RC, HHI), Lerner index	Market entry and exit rates
Perception of monopoly	Monopoly is antithetical to competition	Monopoly is the temporary and logical consequence of the competitive process
Perception of concentration	Industrial concentration is long-lasting and has its roots in the anti-competitive practices of firms	Industrial concentration is the result of the superior efficiency of large firms
Consequences of concentration	Rising prices and decreasing pace of innovation; unjustified profits	Lower production costs; high profits for efficient firms
Public policy recommendation	Limit industrial concentration Fight against anti-competitive practices (cartels, abuse of dominant position)	Maintain the contestability of the market

These two views are nowadays reflected in the economic debates on industrial concentration at the macroeconomic level, especially in the United States. We have indeed observed that market concentration has increased sharply in the United States since the early 2000s (see Philippon, 2019; Bajgar et al., 2019; Grullon et al., 2018), as evidenced by the evolution of the Herfindahl-Hirschman Index (Figure 9).

Figure 9. The evolution of the HHI in the United States (1972–2014)

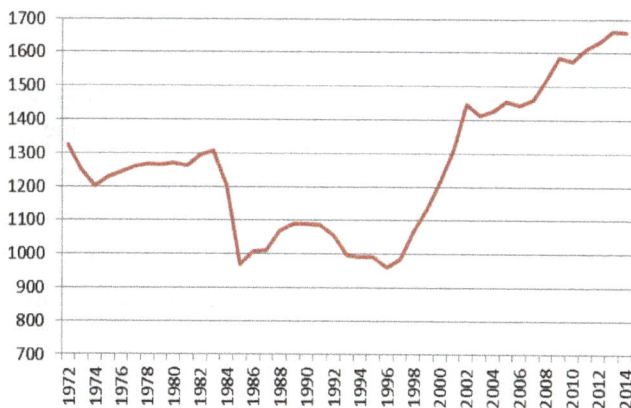

Source: Grullon et al. (2019)

According to Loecker et al. (2020), the margin rate, which was 18% (in relation to marginal cost) in 1980, reached 67% in 2014 (Figure 10).

Figure 10. Evolution of the U.S. business margin rate (1960–2014)

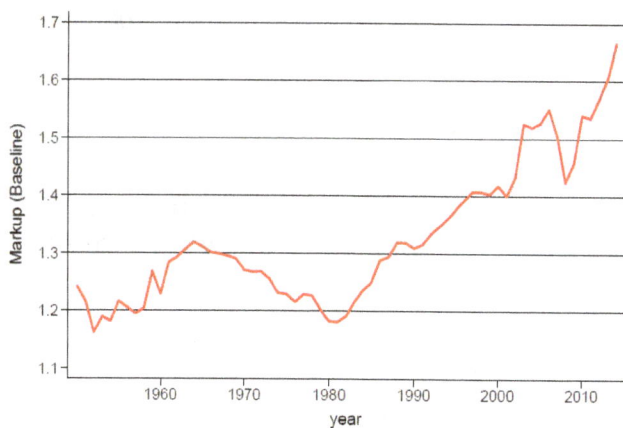

Source: Loecker et al. (2020)

The question then is whether the concomitant increase in concentration and margins is the sign of fierce competition (optimistic approach) or whether it reflects a weakening of competition to the detriment of consumers and welfare (pessimistic approach). In the words of Covarrubias et al. (2019), the question is to separate the "good" concentration from the "bad."

According to the "optimistic" view, market concentration results from the fact that the most productive firms develop more and grow at the expense of the less productive ones; market concentration illustrates a virtuous reallocation process between firms. The increase in margins is the consequence of the fall in production costs.

Autor et al. (2019) thus find that sectors that have experienced the greatest increase in concentration are also those in which productivity and innovation are the most intense.

The fact that competition is driving market concentration and higher margins is due to a combination of different forces:

- The digital economy has reduced the "search costs" for consumers. They can more easily compare products and arbitrate in favor of firms that offer the best products or are the most efficient (firms Autor et al. call "superstar firms"). Put in more technical terms, consumers have become more price elastic as supply substitution increases. We must therefore observe a decline in the least efficient firms, which are no longer "isolated" from competition by geographical distance, and a concomitant increase in the market share of firms that offer the best products.

- The digital economy is characterized by strong network effects,[9] which lead to a winner-take-all phenomenon. The more users a firm has today, the more likely it will conquer new consumers tomorrow.

---

9   See Chapter 4.

- Many activities are based on the accumulation of intangible capital (software, R&D) that can be duplicated on a very large scale without additional marginal cost. Economies of scale are therefore particularly high. In particular, a firm's growth does not require a significant increase in the number of employees; the more a firm grows, the smaller its footprint in terms of jobs will be.

In the same vein, we can also observe an increase in concentration and a drop in margins in certain sectors. These two facts are the sign of market contestability. Thus, in the case of retail, opening up to competition with low-cost countries requires domestic producers to increase their size in order to lower their costs and resist imports: market concentration is higher, but margins are low. For instance, the market share of Walmart has increased since the early 2000s, but its margin rate has decreased.

According to the "pessimistic" thesis, industrial concentration and high margin rates express a lack of competition in the domestic market. Thus, Covarrubias et al. (2019) and Philippon (2019) mobilize several indicators to challenge the optimistic thesis. They note that since the early 2000s, the United States has experienced:

- A decline in the exit rate of firms, while the process of creative destruction should lead to the exit of the least efficient firms

- A negative correlation between changes in market concentration and changes in productivity

- A positive correlation between changes in market concentration and price changes in markets such as cell phones, retail banking, and air transport

- A decline in private investment at the aggregate level and leading firms' level – this fact is contrary to the idea that leading firms compete strongly with each other, which encourages them to invest

– A decline in market share turbulence among industry leaders – which is consistent with the view that economies of scale and network effects help maintain incumbent positions; however, this is also consistent with the pessimistic view that leading firms are protected from competition by barriers to entry.

The authors conclude that the above indicators rather support the thesis of a "bad concentration" which would have developed from the 2000s. This does not exclude that in certain sectors, such as retail and computers, there may be "good" concentration, resulting essentially from the pressure exerted by international competition.

Table 4. The two theses on industrial concentration in the United States

Variables	"Good concentration" thesis	"Poor concentration" thesis
Exit rate of firms	Rate increase	Lowering the rate
Correlation between change in market concentration and change in total factor productivity	Positive correlation	Negative correlation
Correlation between changes in market concentration and price changes	Negative correlation	Positive correlation
Overall investment rate	Rate increase	Lowering the rate
Investment rate among leaders	Rate increase	Lowering the rate
Turnover rate of leaders in a sector	Undetermined effect	Lowering the rate

In reality, "superstar" firms initially drove productivity gains in the U.S. economy and then turned into "fading stars," protected by artificial regulations resulting from their lobbying activity, anti-competitive mergers, and low antitrust scrutiny.

This "bad" concentration would result in excessive market power for large firms, to the detriment of consumers and welfare (via price increases) but also of employees (via monopsony situations in the labor market). The main winners of this industrial concentration would be the shareholders, through the redistribution of dividends or the increase in share value. This critical view of concentration implies a corrective intervention by the public authorities, notably through the return of antitrust policy in the United States.

Chapter 3

Competition in Action: its Micro and Macroeconomic Effects

After presenting the two main perspectives on competition, it is interesting to review its main effects, as observed in practice by economists. The methodology employed most frequently involves comparing a market's situation before and after it experiences a "competitive shock." Competitive shocks come in many different forms: the entry of a new *low-cost* business model, a patent expiry, an increase in imports from a low-cost country, or the opening up of a sector, to name a few.

We begin by examining the effects of increased competition on demand before focusing on its impact on supply and adopting both a microeconomic and macroeconomic perspective.

I. Effects on Demand

1. The Effect on Prices and Quantities

The best-known and most immediate effect of strong competition is a fall in price. This fall concerns not only the prices charged by new entrants but also the prices that all firms in the market charge as they adapt their pricing policies.

The magnitude of this effect depends on different parameters, such as:

- *The nature of the entrant.* When the entrant is a low-cost firm or has a frugal business model (e.g., an online seller with no physical stores), the effect on prices can be substantial.

- *The situation before the entry.* The transition from a monopoly to a duopoly situation should lead to a sharper drop in prices than if the market already had many firms.

- *The degree of product differentiation.* The more substitutable the products, the greater the entry's effect on price.

- *The size of the entrant.* If the entrant enters with high capacity, the impact on price will be significant.

A first illustrative example is the impact the entry of a generic firm can have on the price of a brand-name drug (called "princeps") after its patent has expired. In the case of pharmaceuticals, the firm holding a patent enjoys strong market power because it benefits from temporary market exclusivity. The price of the original drug is therefore temporarily higher than the cost of production, including R&D. Once the patent has expired, however, generic firms will copy the drug, and they do not have to bear the R&D costs. We can therefore expect a significant price reduction compared to the initial price.

In a 2019 study of 95 molecules that lost their patents in the United States during the period spanning from 1994 to 2003, Castanheira et al. analyze the price evolution of a drug after its patent has expired. Figure 11 plots the drug's average price before and after patent expiration, which occurs at date $t = 0$. The y-axis shows that the price (normalized to 1 at the start) remains fairly stable in the 12 quarters before patent expiry. But from the date $t = 0$, the price decreases quite rapidly; one year after patent expiry, the price has fallen on average by 30%, and this fall reaches 50% over a period of three years (i.e., 12 quarters).

Figure 11. Evolution of prices and quantities after the entry of a generic

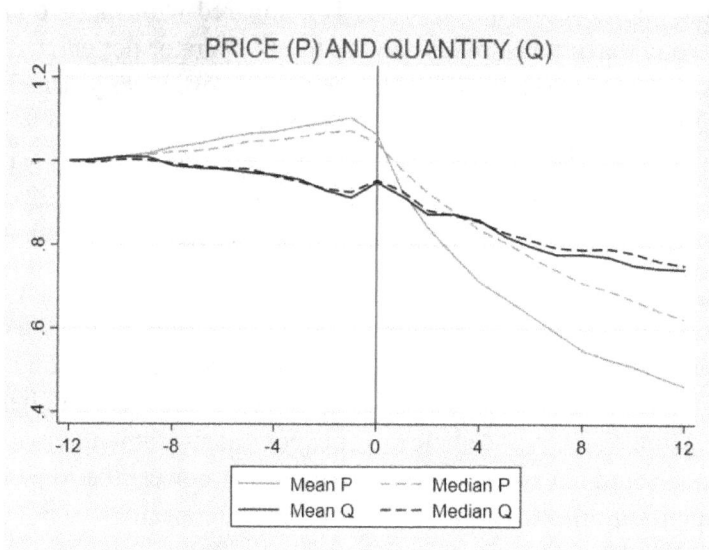

Note: The x-axis is expressed in quarters.
Source: Castanheira et al. (2019)

It should be noted that this decrease in the generic price does not exclude an increase in the price of the princeps. We can explain this situation, described as the "generic paradox," by the fact that there are two markets for the same drug, with two types of consumers. On the one hand, there are those who stay "loyal" to the original drug because they consider the quality of the princeps to be superior. On the other hand, there are price-sensitive patients who consider the generic to be of the same quality as the princeps. After the entry of a generic, the princeps producer can react by increasing its price in order to recover in margin what it has lost in volume.

A second illustrative example is the 2012 entry of a fourth mobile phone operator, Free Mobile, in France. A 2014 study by UFC Que Choisir measured the impact this entry had on prices, based on the so-called counterfactual method, wherein the observed evolution of mobile phone subscription prices is compared with the evolution that would have taken place had the fourth operator not entered the market. The observed decline in mobile bills over two years (2012 and 2013) was 30%, down from an average of €24.1 to €16.9. The counterfactual decline in the absence of Free Mobile's entry would have been 9%, with the average bill falling from €24.1 to €22. The decrease due solely to the entry of a fourth operator would be 21% over two years.

We can see that the price decrease is not only attributable to the new entrant. The three other competing operators also reacted by lowering their prices and launching their own *low-cost* offers shortly before Free Mobile's entry (see below). This point is fundamental in order to understand consumers' gain in purchasing power: the impact of competition on prices does not only benefit consumers who have moved to the new entrant; it also indirectly (but to a lesser extent) benefits consumers of incumbent firms.

A third example is the 2012 entry of a new firm into the high-speed Italian rail market. As noted by the French Transport Regulation Authority (ART) in 2018, *"the mere announcement of the entry of a competitor resulted in a significant decrease in the incumbent's ticket prices, before the actual entry of the new operator. In particular, the incumbent reduced its average ticket price on the Milan–Rome route by 31% between 2011 and 2012, some months before the launch of the new entrant's services in April 2012. After the launch, prices continued to fall more moderately.*" (free translation).

As soon as a price falls in these markets, the quantity demanded increases. As we saw in Chapter 1, the demand for a good is a decreasing function of its price.

Thus, since Italian high-speed passenger rail transport opened to competition, there has been a jump in train ridership. Indeed, following the 2012 entry of NTV in the face of the incumbent operator Trenitalia, the number of high-speed train passengers increased by 49% between 2012 and 2015, to the benefit of both railway companies (24% for the incumbent operator and 355% for the new entrant).

The price drop's impact on quantities depends on the price elasticity of demand:[10] The more price-elastic demand is, the greater the impact on quantities. The value of price elasticity varies, particularly according to the type of consumers and the needs that must be satisfied.

For example, it is usual to distinguish at least two reasons for passenger air transport: *business* and *leisure*. The price elasticity for the business travel motive is low: 0.27 (in absolute value) for long-haul flights and 0.7 (in absolute value) for short/medium-haul flights. Conversely, the elasticity for the leisure travel motive is higher: 1.04 (in absolute terms) for long-haul flights and 1.52 (in absolute terms) for short/medium-haul flights. Therefore, a price reduction will have less effect on volumes if the airline targets business people. Conversely, low-cost airlines mainly carry a leisure

---

10   For a definition, see note 1.

clientele, and benefit from a strong growth in volumes when they reduce the ticket price. These additional volumes come mainly from people who did not previously fly. This phenomenon is known as an *induction effect*: the price reduction creates additional traffic. For example, on the London–Barcelona route, the 1995 entry of EasyJet – in the face of the Iberia–British Airways duopoly – led to a fivefold increase in traffic in ten years. This induction effect concerns both the low-cost airline and the legacy airline, which, by lowering its prices, has also attracted new clients.

When analyzing the impact of a price decrease on demand, it is important to reason "all other things being equal." Indeed, the demand can decrease when the price decreases if factors other than price intervene at the same time. In their 2019 study of generic entry, Castanheira et al. found that generic entry leads to a decrease in the price of the drug – and also in the quantities (Figure 11). This is because the patent holder implements a strategy of *evergreening*, which entails launching a second generation of the drug just before the patent expiry on the first drug. As a result, some patients will turn to the new version of the drug.

As soon as competition lowers market prices and increases the quantities, consumers obtain a double gain (Figure 12):

- Consumers who previously consumed at price P_1 now pay a lower price P_2. They benefit from a transfer of surplus from producers, equal to rectangle A.

- Consumers who did not consume at price P_1 but who consume at price P_2 obtain a surplus equal to area B.

The increase in competition therefore leads to a total increase in consumer surplus equal to the area (A + B).

Figure 12. The two effects of price reduction

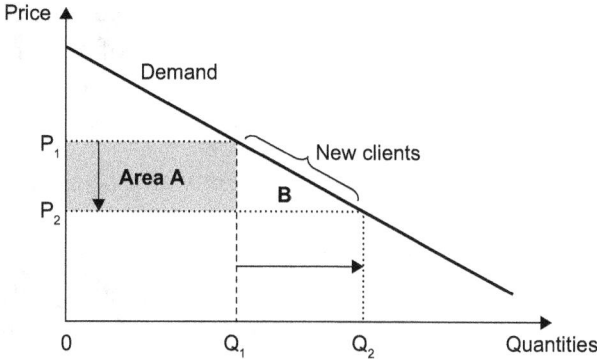

When reliable empirical data on price decline and volumes are available, we can quantitatively estimate the gain for consumers resulting from an increase in competition. For example, in the case of the entry of Free Mobile, UFC Que Choisir (2014) estimated that the total gain for consumers was approximately €6.8 billion over two years.

2. The Effect on Product Quality and Diversity

Concerning product quality, logic would conclude that an increase in competition would force incumbent firms to better take into account the needs of consumers who now have the choice of going elsewhere. Anecdotally, it has sometimes been argued that the entry of Uber into the passenger transport market after 2010 has led taxis to improve their quality of service (see Wallsten, 2015).

More scientifically, several empirical studies have measured the impact of an increase in competition on product quality.

For example, in food retail, Matsa (2009) analyzed the influence that a Walmart store opening had on the out-of-stock rate of competing stores in the same catchment area. When a store is not threatened by the competition of Walmart, it has a high out-of-stock rate since consumers have no alternatives. Matsa found that the entry of a Walmart store reduces the out-of-stock rate by 24%; competing stores better stock their shelves to dissuade consumers from going to Walmart.

In passenger air transport, the primary quality criterion is flight safety. Some claim that the increase in competition since the 1990s has been detrimental to flight safety. However, the entry of low-cost airlines has not altered the long-term downward trend in the fatality rate. Brown (2017) showed, through a sample of American flights spanning the period 1995–2005, that the number of accidents decreases by more than 70% when a flight is operated by a low-cost airline. This result can be explained by the fact that low-cost airlines are young and therefore extremely protective of their reputation. A fatal accident could bankrupt them. Moreover, there is a link between the accident rate and the company's financial health; major low-cost airlines are in good financial health.

Quality in air transport can also be measured in terms of flight punctuality. To what extent does the intensity of competition on a route affect punctuality? Based on a sample of more than 800,000 flights in the United States, Mazzeo (2003) investigated the various factors that explain flight arrival delays, including weather conditions, the degree of airport congestion, the aircraft characteristics (age, size), and the market share concentration on each route. Mazzeo showed that routes with a monopoly or a high market share concentration have a higher proportion of delayed flights: competition increases punctuality. Greenfield (2014) conducted a more recent study on 100 U.S. airports that reached a similar conclusion: increasing market share concentration at an airport is correlated with an increase in flight delay rates.

Intermodal competition between rail and air can also improve punctuality. For example, Fang et al. (2020) analyzed the impact of the launch of high-speed train lines from Beijing on the punctuality of flights operating on the same routes. In their study, they compared airlines that were subject to train competition with those that were not. Using a database of more than 865,000 flights traveling from Beijing to 113 domestic destinations, they showed that the launch of high-speed rail has positively impacted the punctuality of airlines operating on the same routes, particularly through a reduction of departure delays.

In the passenger rail transport sector, an improvement in service quality has also been observed in Europe following the opening up to competition, even though there is currently no synthetic quality indicator. The ART (2018) states:

> The existence of a situation of competition between opera-tors is usually accompanied by a quantitative and qualitative improvement in the services offered, whether in the context of competition (for the market) for contracted services or competition (in the market) for non-contracted services. In Germany, liberalization has resulted in a large-scale renewal of the rolling stock fleet, so that the average age of the DB fleet fell from 17.3 years to 7.5 years between 1997 and 2015. In Italy, upon entering high-speed train services, the new entrant sought to innovate in terms of onboard service quality by introducing free Wi-Fi, multimedia services, and high-end catering. In the end, both the new entrant and the incumbent have developed complementary bus, car rental, and car-sharing services. The two companies have also extended their service offerings in stations (free translation).

Concerning rail safety, opening up to competition has not had a negative impact. On the contrary, European countries that have opened up their domestic rail passenger markets to competition are among the safest. For example, relative to the level of their rail traffic, the United Kingdom and Germany have fewer train accidents than France.

The quality of products may also be related to their environmental characteristics. A 2021 study by Aghion et al. showed that competition could improve the environmental quality of products. Indeed, at first sight, the effect of competition on pollution seems detrimental: by lowering prices, competition leads to an increase in consumption and consequently an increase in polluting emissions. However, the opposite effect can also occur. As soon as consumers are sensitive to environmental criteria, competition will encourage suppliers to launch "clean" products in order to differentiate themselves from others. In a monopoly situation, a firm would have little incentive to take into account consumers' environmental preferences, as consumers have no other options. The authors tested this hypothesis on a sample of car manufacturers in 41 countries and showed that the propensity to file "green" patents increased with the intensity of competition in the local market.

In addition to its impact on product quality, competition can also increase the variety of products available on the market, allowing each consumer to "find the right product." The impact on consumers of greater product variety can be analyzed in two different ways:

- A first approach considers that the consumer's utility increases with the number of varieties. For example, a consumer will find greater satisfaction by consuming 200 grams of five varieties of fruits – i.e., a total quantity of 1 kilo – than by consuming 1 kilo of a single fruit. Competition often results in the entry of new firms that offer products that differ from the existing ones ;

- A second approach assumes that each consumer wishes to consume an ideal product variety. Consumers' utility increases when they can consume a product close to their ideal. But not all consumers have the same ideal variety. In a single-product monopoly situation, some consumers are likely to be dissatisfied since the product the monopoly offers will be far from their ideal product. By enlarging the number of products available, competition allows each consumer to get closer to their ideal product.

- This impact of competition on product variety has been observed in many markets open to competition. In air transport, for example, low-cost carriers in Europe have increased the density of the route network, particularly by linking small cities directly to each other. According to the European Commission, the number of destinations served in Europe rose from 2,700 in 1992 to 7,400 in 2016, mainly due to the entry of low-cost airlines. This has resulted in a strong increase in the connectivity between European regions, favoring especially southern regions (Andalusia, Sicily, etc.).

Similarly, in rail transport, the opening of competition in Europe has led to an increase in territorial coverage, with the reopening of lines, and in frequency. For example, the ART (2018) notes that *"the liberalization of rail passenger transport services has been accompanied in Germany, the United Kingdom, and Sweden by a significant increase in their attractiveness (measured by changes in passenger-kilometer ridership) since the opening. In Germany, ridership has increased by 29%. In Great Britain, ridership has more than doubled over the period 1994–2015. In Sweden, ridership increased by 80% between 1988 and 2013."* (free translation).

II. Supply-Side Effects

In addition to its effects on demand, competition also has some impacts on supply. It encourages incumbent firms to reposition their products, sometimes even by adopting a business model similar to that of the new entrant (1). Competition also has important effects on productivity and innovation (2). These various supply-side effects will impact the labor market, both in terms of employment and wages (3).

1. Repositioning the Products

When the intensity of competition in a market changes significantly, particularly after the entry of a new firm, incumbent firms will react not only by adjusting their prices, but also by repositioning their offer. The whole configuration of the market will be affected by the entry of a new competitor.

A first form of repositioning consists of duplicating the new entrant's business model in order to "fight with the same weapons." For example, when the entrant is a low-cost firm, the incumbent can react by launching its own low-cost product. In the mobile phone market, prior to Free Mobile's entry, the three major operators (Bouygues Telecom, Orange, and SFR) offered postpaid subscriptions in the form of a bundle (SIM card + mobile phone) with a long-time commitment (of 12 or 24 months). In January 2012, Free Mobile entered the market by breaking radically with this model. It offered only a few packages, all of which were not tied to time commitments and were centered around the SIM card only, the telephone being bought separately. The irruption of this low-cost offer led the three incumbent firms to react by also offering subscriptions without a phone and time commitment contract.

Moreover, the three incumbents countered Free Mobile by launching their own low-cost brand, which we term *fighting brands*. A study by Bourreau et al. (2018) shows that these low-cost offers would probably not have been launched without the entry of Free Mobile, as low-cost offers would have simply cannibalized the three incumbents' sales on their high-cost offers, reducing profits. On the other hand, by launching these offers, the three operators limited their profits decline by containing the new entrant's market share. The authors break down the impact that Free Mobile's entry had on consumer surplus into three distinct effects:

- A variety effect, which led some consumers to choose Free Mobile's low-cost offer

- A competition effect, which forced the incumbent operators to lower the price of their existing high-cost offers

- A low-price effect due to the three incumbents' launch of low-cost brands. Out of an estimated €4.5 billion increase in consumer surplus over the 2012–2014 period, the launch of low-cost brands accounted for 31% of the gain, far ahead of the effect of lower prices on existing high-cost packages.

Beyond the case of the mobile phone market, we can observe this type of repositioning in most sectors marked by the entry of a low-cost firm. Particularly in air transport, the shock constituted in Europe by the rise of low-cost companies such as EasyJet or Ryanair has led incumbent airlines to adopt certain characteristics of the low-cost model – or even to become low-cost themselves. This strategy has most often taken the form of a "split." Part of the business is transferred to a low-cost subsidiary (point-to-point flights in the medium-haul market), while the rest of the business (long-haul and hub-feeding flights) continues to follow a more traditional model. This duplication can consist, for example, of buying a low-cost airline, as the IAG group (British Airways) did when it took control of the low-cost airline Vueling in 2013. Another solution has been to create a new dedicated subsidiary within the incumbent airline; for example, Air France-KLM launched its own low-cost subsidiary, Transavia France, in 2007.

A second – quite radical – form of repositioning is to *exit* the market after the entry of a new firm. This may occur when the new entrant has such an efficient cost structure that the incumbent cannot compete.

For example, suppose a high-cost airline has a unit cost of 10 cents per kilometer and is in a monopoly situation. In this case, it will charge a monopoly price of 13 cents. A low-cost firm enters the market with a unit cost of 3 cents per kilometer and charges a monopoly price of 8 cents per kilometer. In economics, this scenario is called a *drastic innovation* (Tirole, 2015) – the monopoly price of the new firm is lower than the marginal cost of the incumbent firm. Unless it too adopts a low-cost model, the incumbent firm has no choice but to exit the market, since the lowest price it can charge is 10 cents (i.e., a price higher than the entrant's monopoly price). In this case, a high-cost monopoly is replaced by a low-cost monopoly.

2. The Effect on Productivity and Innovation

When firms are forced to compete continuously, competition becomes an important source of productivity gains. The impact of competition on productivity can be measured empirically in several ways.

A first method consists of comparing markets with different competitive intensities in order to check whether competitive markets have higher productivity levels. There have been numerous empirical studies, all of which led to a fairly clear conclusion (for a summary, see CMA, 2015): high concentration in a sector has a negative effect on labor productivity or overall factor productivity. For example, the OECD analyzed the relationship between a product market regulation (PMR) indicator and productivity in a study of countries, concluding that sectors with high entry regulation had more limited productivity gains. Bourlès et al. (2013) applied a similar reasoning to intermediate products; in a study of 15 OECD countries over the period spanning from 1985 to 2007, the authors showed that a strong restriction on competition in upstream markets had a negative effect on downstream productivity. In the case of services, the French Treasury carried out a study in 2009 on a sample of 11 OECD countries, and 20 sectors showed a decreasing relationship in the services sector between the markup rate (an indirect indicator of the intensity of competition) and the productivity growth rate.

A second method is to study the impact of a competitive shock on productivity. For example, we can analyze the evolution of a firm's productivity when it moves from a legal monopoly to a competitive situation. In 2011, Bridgman and Gomes studied the productivity evolution of Brazilian oil firm Petrobras – which had a legal monopoly until 1995 – before the firm was subjected to competition. The authors showed that the introduction of competition led to a strong increase in the firm's productivity: while it increased by 4.6% on average between 1976 and 1994, it grew by 13% each year after 1995 (Figure 13). This evolution was due to internal reforms that could have been implemented before 1995, including the shutdown of the least efficient wells, but which the firm had no incentive to carry out since it was not threatened by competition. Similarly, in a 2005 study of the North American iron ore mining industry, Schmitz observed that the opening up to foreign competition in the 1980s led American operators to achieve very strong productivity gains in order to resist Brazilian imports.

Generally speaking, studies on the impact of the liberalization of a highly regulated sector – such as gas, electricity, water, transportation, and communications – conclude that there have been strong increases in productivity (see, for example, Fabrizio et al., 2007, on electricity).

Figure 13. Impact of the introduction of competition on Petrobras's productivity (1976–2001)

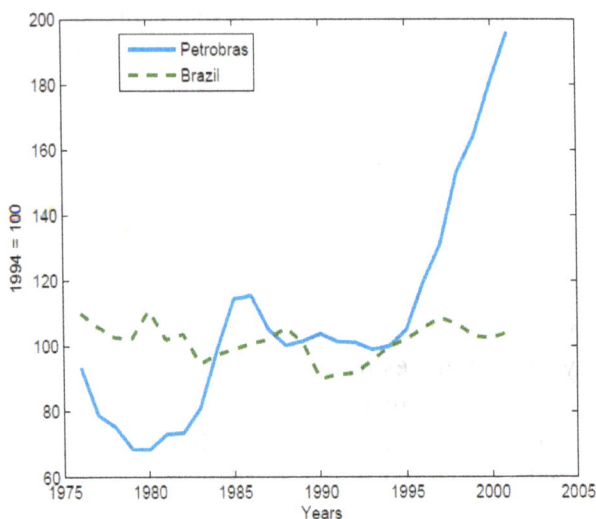

Source: Bridgman and Gomes (2011)

If there is a positive relationship between the intensity of competition and productivity, the origins of this relationship remain to be explored.

The first cause is internal to firms. Competition exerts a "disciplinary" function on managers, who must constantly compare their performances to, and justify them against, those of their competitors. Competition therefore reduces the temptation to let production costs drift; strong competition in the product market encourages firms to adopt more efficient management methods.

A second cause is external to firms and involves a process of firms' selection: those with the highest levels of productivity will gradually replace those that are less efficient. There is then a reallocation of market shares between firms, within a sector and between sectors. Empirical studies confirm that this selection effect is quantitatively more important than the internal discipline effect. In the United States, for example, half of the productivity growth in the manufacturing sector during the 1990s and 2000s came from the entry of new firms and the exit of less efficient firms (Foster et al., 2001). Moreover, the entry of new firms has a "contestability" effect on incumbent firms, encouraging them to become more productive and renew their business models. Bartelsman et al. (2004) showed that the higher a sector's rate of firm renewal, the higher the productivity of incumbent firms.

In France, a 2019 study by Ben Hassine pointed out that productivity gains following the 2008 crisis were driven by a process of reallocation of market shares to the most efficient firms and by a *cleansing effect*, leading to the decline of the least productive firms.

Productivity is not just about producing the same products at a lower cost. It can also mean making a technological leap towards new products or production processes. The central question is whether increased competition is conducive to innovation.

With the standard approach, any increase in competition is beneficial to innovation; since profits in competition are low, firms have a strong incentive to innovate. This is Arrow's (1962) famous *laurel effect* (see Chapter 1). Conversely, following Schumpeter (1943), we can consider that concentrated markets are more conducive to innovation insofar as firms have the financial capabilities to innovate and can more easily appropriate the results of their efforts.

To reconcile these two antinomic approaches, Aghion et al. (2001) assumed that technical progress is a step-by-step process (and not a process wherein new entrants replace incumbents); firms are more or less behind the technological frontier, defined as the highest level of performance. The effect of increased competition on innovation will differ greatly depending on the firms' initial positions. For those close to the technological frontier, increased competition will encourage them to innovate more in order to "escape competition." Conversely, increased competition will discourage firms that are already far from the technological frontier, and they will not be able to catch up.

A 2009 empirical study by Aghion et al. on the British case confirmed the relationship between the intensity of competition in a sector (measured by the penetration rate of foreign firms) and innovation (measured by the number of patents the firm filed). In Figure 14, the top curve corresponds to firms close to the technology frontier; the bottom curve represents firms far from the technological frontier. We see that firms initially close to the technological frontier react positively to an increase in competition by innovating more to "stay in the race." Conversely, firms initially far from the technological frontier react negatively by being discouraged from catching up.

**Figure 14. Innovation and competition by distance
from the technological frontier**

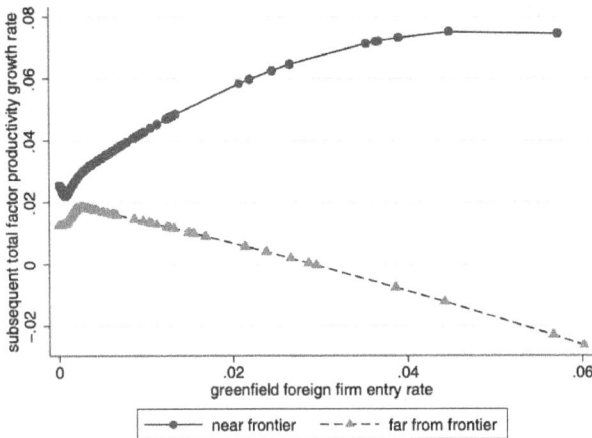

Source: Aghion et al. (2009)

If we now reason at the aggregate level, the effect of competition on innovation (and growth) takes the form of an inverted U (Figure 15).

When the intensity of competition is low (left-hand side of Figure 15), firms initially far from the frontier have a strong incentive to join it, as their profits will increase significantly if they do. Conversely, firms at the frontier have little incentive to escape competition. It follows that when the intensity of competition is initially low, increased competition will have a positive effect on innovation.

Conversely, when the intensity of competition is initially high (right-hand side of Figure 15), firms on the frontier want to innovate to escape their competitors. The technological frontier will thus shift, leaving most firms far behind this new frontier. However, the firms far from the frontier react negatively to increased competition. It follows that when the intensity of competition is initially high, increased competition has a negative effect on innovation.

Figure 15. Incentives to innovate and competition: an inverted U-shaped relationship

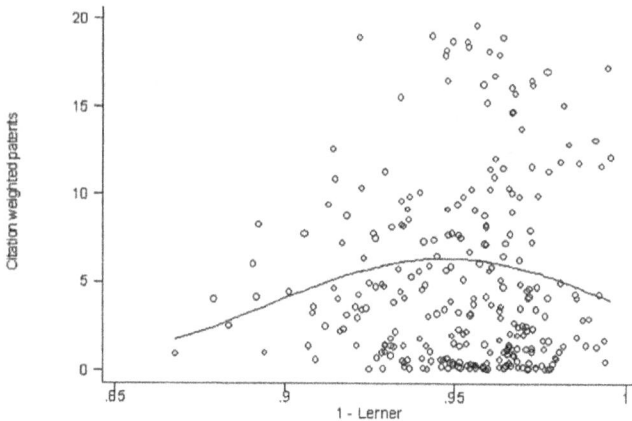

Source: Aghion et al. (2005)

This result has two important empirical consequences:

- In international trade, when a country opens up to exports and imports, there will be more competition among firms. This greater exposure to international competition will stimulate innovation in the most productive firms and discourage innovation in firms positioned far from the technological frontier.

- In terms of growth, the closer a country is to the technological frontier – i.e., the closer its productivity is to that of the most productive country, the United States – the more competition favors innovation and growth. Indeed, the closer a country is to the technological frontier, the more firms in that country are close to the frontier compared to firms far from the frontier, and the greater the incentive to innovate outweighs the discouragement effect.

III. Effects on Employment

Competition is often perceived as a job-killing process: the entry of new firms undermines existing firms, which reduces their production, resulting in the laying off of some employees. In reality, the mechanisms at work are more complex insofar as the effects of competition on employment are both direct and indirect.

1. The Effect on the Volume of Employment

The entry of a new competitor with a more efficient business model can be considered a productivity shock. The new firm lowers prices and gains market share – to the detriment of the incumbents, which must adjust their production downwards. The "creative destruction" in the product market is then transposed onto the labor market – there is a process of job destruction/creation through the reallocation of jobs from incumbent firms to newcomers (Figure 16).

Figure 16. Entry and intrasectoral reallocation of jobs

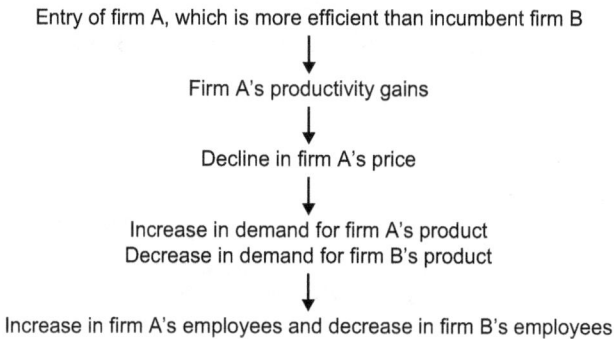

Entry of firm A, which is more efficient than incumbent firm B

↓

Firm A's productivity gains

↓

Decline in firm A's price

↓

Increase in demand for firm A's product
Decrease in demand for firm B's product

↓

Increase in firm A's employees and decrease in firm B's employees

Insofar as the new entrants are more efficient, there is a risk that the employment balance will be negative within the sector, i.e., for the same volume of production, the newcomer will employ fewer workers than the incumbent firm. In the case of air transport, for instance, the productivity of a low-cost firm is on average two to three times higher than that of an incumbent firm. At constant demand, we should therefore expect total employment to fall as low-cost carriers gain market shares. However, this is not what has been observed in Europe. During the period spanning from 1998 to 2010, marked by the strong growth of low-cost carriers, direct employment in air transport remained almost stable at around 420,000 jobs.

This is because productivity gains result in price cuts, which in turn stimulate demand. For example, if a low-cost firm is twice as productive per employee as an incumbent, and if demand for air transport doubles as a result of the lower ticket price, there will be a transfer of jobs from the incumbent to the low-cost firm, but without any net job destruction. As we saw earlier, this traffic induction effect is particularly strong in air transport, especially for tourists, who are very price sensitive; as the price elasticity of demand is high, the increase in demand offsets the negative effect that productivity has on employment (Figure 17).

Figure 17. The direct and indirect effect of competition on intrasector employment

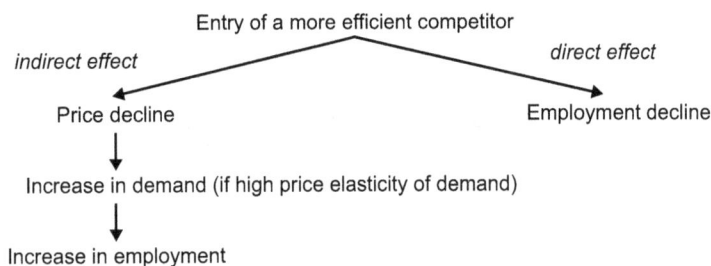

Entry of a more efficient competitor

indirect effect   *direct effect*

Price decline   Employment decline

Increase in demand (if high price elasticity of demand)

Increase in employment

It could be argued that this reasoning on the intrasectoral reallocation of jobs only applies in a closed economy. But if we consider an open economy, an intensification of competition can be detrimental to domestic employment and beneficial to jobs located abroad. This is the case, for example, when a sector is opened up to imports, particularly from a low-cost country. Imports will lead firms to reduce their production and therefore lay off workers, without transferring jobs to the domestic level.

Thus, Autor et al. (2013) showed an inverse relationship between the penetration rate of Chinese imports in the United States and American industrial employment. They show that the U.S. regions where industries have been most affected by Chinese imports have experienced the largest decline in industrial employment. According to Acemoglu et al. (2016), increased competition resulting from Chinese imports led to the loss of 2 million jobs in the United States during the period spanning from 1995 to 2011.

One might be tempted to conclude that opening up to trade with low-cost countries only destroys jobs, especially for low-skilled workers. But in reality, a country's openness often works both ways: in exchange for greater openness to imports in sector A, the country will negotiate greater openness to exports in sector B, which will result in job creation. The net job balance of trade openness thus depends on the difference between import-related job destruction and export-related job creation. Feenstra et al. (2017) and Feenstra and Sasahara (2017) measured U.S. job destruction and creation over the period spanning from 1995 to 2011. For Chinese import-related destruction, they find a similar order of magnitude to Acemoglu et al. (2016) – roughly 2 million jobs. However, the authors also show that in sectors such as semiconductors, oil refinement, and car engines, export growth has been strong, leading to job creation in some U.S. regions. In addition, U.S. exports have created service-related jobs – between 700,000 and 4 million, depending on the simulations. As a result, the net effect of trade openness to China on U.S. employment – despite the growth of Chinese imports from the 2000s onwards – is positive.

Apart from the reallocation of jobs within the same sector, the entry of new competitors may also have a positive impact on employment in other sectors. Indeed, the entry of a more efficient competitor results in an increase in consumer purchasing power, which stimulates demand for other products – particularly those complementary to the one whose price has fallen (Figure 18). Once again, low-cost air travel is a particularly interesting case. The gain resulting from the reduction in plane ticket prices led many passengers to book higher-quality accommodations; this new expenditure has boosted employment in hotels and restaurants.

However, this intersectoral reallocation of jobs presupposes a work-force that is mobile between sectors and regions. However, employees are imperfectly mobile, both in terms of skills and geography. Under these conditions, a competitive shock may result in an increase in structural unemployment. In particular, in the case of a massive and rapid opening up to international trade, a country risks bearing strong "adjustment costs" in the geographical areas affected by imported products. Autor and al. (2016) studied the local effects of the "China shock" on the U.S. labor market and found that the decline in employment in the most exposed regions was not offset by an increase in the geographical mobility of workers. They found that the regions affected had become entrenched in the economic downturn and did not appear to have fully recovered, even ten years after the shock. The fact that these localized effects persisted for at least a decade suggests that the adjustment costs of trade shocks can be high in the labor market in the absence of responsive public policies. The role of public authorities is to remove the obstacles to worker retraining by setting up effective mechanisms for vocational reskilling and geographical mobility.

Figure 18. Competition and intersectoral reallocation of employment

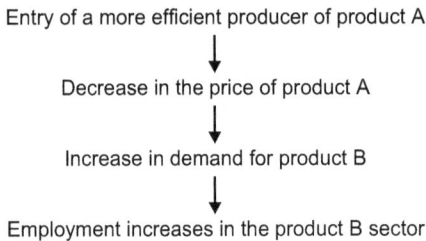

Entry of a more efficient producer of product A

↓

Decrease in the price of product A

↓

Increase in demand for product B

↓

Employment increases in the product B sector

To conclude, the net effect of a competitive shock on the overall employment volume must include all the direct and indirect effects we have described. Overall, empirical studies generally conclude that the net effect on employment is positive. For example, Basker (2005) showed that the arrival of a Walmart store in a U.S. locality leads, in both the short and long term, to a net increase in employment in the retail sector. In the short term, each new store created 100 new jobs; over a five-year period, taking into account the closure of competing stores, the net gain amounts to 50 jobs per store. This calculation includes the negative effects of Walmart's entry – essentially, the closure of small stores and a decline in employment in the wholesale sector, which is negatively affected by Walmart's strong bargaining power.

2. Effects on Wages

While empirical studies fail to identify an overall negative impact of competition on employment, competition can have several impacts on wages.

First, increased competition will have a differential effect on wages, depending on the initial situation in the labor market.

If the workforce is limited by entry barriers, such as a numerus clausus, labor scarcity will likely lead to wages being higher than their competitive level. As a result, increased competition – e.g., lower barriers to entry – will lead to lower wages. For example, in the U.S. road transport industry, before the 1980's deregulation, employees of unionized firms earned on average almost 50% more than employees of non-unionized firms. After the industry was opened up to competition, the unions' power declined sharply, leading to a decline in the wage gap (see Rose, 1987). The reason for this decrease is that the new entrants decided to outsource labor and not to recognize the power of unions.

Conversely, a situation wherein the demand for labor is concentrated in the hands of a few firms will lead to wages dropping lower than their competitive level; firms will take advantage of their monopsony position to "exploit" the workforce. As we saw in Chapter 1, this is not a theoretical situation, particularly in some U.S. labor markets. Therefore, increased competition between firms is rather good news for workers – it leads to both higher wages and higher employment.[11]

In the same vein, some anti-competitive labor market practices can lead to situations in which wages are below their competitive level (see OECD, 2019b; Naidu and Posner, 2018). For example, firms may force workers to sign non-compete clauses, which limit their mobility. According to Colvin and Shierholz (2019), 28% of U.S. private sector workers were reported to have signed such clauses in 2019, up from 18% in 2014. It is interesting to note that these clauses do not only concern highly educated people; they also affect low-skilled workers. Abolishing these clauses should logically lead to increased competition between firms, which would benefit workers.

Firms in the same sector or employment area can also agree to fix wages and/or working conditions, and to refrain from poaching each other's labor. In particular, *no-poaching agreements* – whereby several firms agree to abstain from soliciting, hiring, or recruiting the workers of other firms – are widespread in the United States in sectors such as restaurant franchise chains. According to Ashenfelter and Krueger (2018), this type of clause is present in 58% of the contracts of franchisors such as McDonald's or Burger King.

Since as early as 2010, the U.S. antitrust authorities have been investigating this type of agreement in the high-tech, nursing, and modeling sectors. The fight against this type of anti-competitive agreement should lead to increased competition between firms in the labor market, which will benefit workers through better wages or working conditions.

---

11   This also explains why an increase in the minimum wage can have a positive effect on employment. When the labor market is in a monopsony situation, the wage charged is "too low" to attract enough labor. An increase in this wage then leads to an increase in the level of employment. For a study on the United States, see Azar et al. (2019).

A second effect of competition on wages is that increased competition may lead to higher wage inequality within a country.

To show this, we can start with the famous Heckscher-Ohlin-Samuelson (HOS) theory of international trade. Let's assume two countries (France and Vietnam), which have two factors of production (skilled and unskilled labor), and which produce two goods (aircraft and textiles) in autarky. France is relatively abundant in skilled labor compared to Vietnam. We can suppose that the production of an aircraft involves more skilled labor than that of a textile. Both countries decide to open up to international trade. France, which is relatively abundant in skilled labor, will specialize in the production of aircraft and will export them to Vietnam. Symmetrically, Vietnam, which is relatively abundant in unskilled labor, will specialize in the production of textiles and will export them to France. Following the opening up to international trade, France will increase its demand for skilled labor, which raises the wages of skilled workers; and it will decrease the demand for unskilled labor, which lowers the wages of unskilled workers. The opening up to trade with Vietnam has benefited skilled workers, while unskilled workers lose out. If the wages of unskilled workers cannot adjust downwards (e.g., because of a minimum wage), the opening up to trade will result in higher unemployment of unskilled workers in France. This theoretical result is known as the *Stolper-Samuelson theorem* – openness to international trade increases the remuneration of the factor that is intensively used in the product that is exported, and it decreases the remuneration of the factor that is competed over by imports. In a 2016 empirical study of the "China shock" from the 2000s onwards, Autor et al. observed that U.S. workers located in the sectors most exposed to Chinese imports experienced a decrease in their wages.

Chapter 4

Limits to Competition

As we have seen in the previous chapters, the dynamics of competition require both the entry of new firms and the maintenance of rivalry between incumbent firms. But technological, behavioral, or strategic obstacles can limit the intensity of competition in the market.[12]

First, where economies of scale or network effects are significant, the market will evolve into a situation of oligopoly or "natural" monopoly, which may be difficult to contest. Second, even when many firms are present in a market, it is not certain that consumers will gain an advantage from the competition insofar as their mobility between firms is hampered by information search costs, transfer costs, and behavioral biases. Finally, competition in the market may be limited by the strategic behavior of incumbents, which may engage in cartel practices or abuse of their dominant position.

---

12   There are also political barriers to competition, which we will discuss in Chapter 5.

I. The Role of Technological Barriers

Strong economies of scale or network effects can limit the number of firms in the market and lead to oligopoly or "natural" monopoly situations.

1. Fixed Costs and Natural Monopoly

In some industries, production requires an investment in high fixed costs (e.g., to build infrastructure). The result is that the more a firm produces, the lower its average cost is, because its fixed costs are spread over a larger quantity of products.

For example, suppose a cost function with a constant marginal cost (c) and a fixed cost (F):

$$\text{Total cost} = cQ + F \text{ with } c, F > 0$$

The average cost is obtained by dividing the total cost by the quantities produced:

$$\text{Average cost} = c + F/Q$$

The average cost decreases as the quantity increases and tends asymptotically towards the marginal cost (c).

In such a configuration, it may be efficient for a single firm to supply the entire market in order to obtain the lowest average cost. This situation is called a *natural monopoly*. Indeed, if there are several firms (each with its own infrastructure), the average cost is higher, since each firm can only amortize its fixed cost on a part of the total production.

This situation is found, for example, in industries that require the prior construction of infrastructure throughout a territory before the service can be offered. This is the case of rail transport, which requires a network of tracks, signaling systems, and train stations. Similarly, the water industry requires pipes; the fixed or mobile telephone industry, a network of cables and relay antennas; the gas industry, a network of pipelines; and the electrical industry, a network of high-voltage lines.

A natural monopoly situation poses an economic dilemma. On the one hand, to achieve the lowest average cost, the best solution is to have only one firm in the market. On the other hand, if the firm is in a monopoly situation, it will set a high price – to the detriment of consumers and welfare. To overcome this dilemma, the solution is to accept a monopoly situation but to regulate its market power.

Economic theory has considered several types of regulation of natural monopolies, which can be divided into two main categories: regulation by costs and regulation by prices.

Let's start with the price regulation by costs.

We saw in Chapter 1 that the optimal price for society is a price equal to marginal cost. A first option is to force the monopoly to charge a price equal to marginal cost - this is the *marginal cost pricing* principle. But, because the marginal cost is lower than the average cost, the monopoly will incur losses. In order to compensate the firm for losses, the state may give subsidies to the monopoly.

A second option is that the state sets a price equal to the average cost; in this case, the monopoly will not make any loss – this is the *average cost pricing* principle. In the specific case of a multi-product monopoly, the Ramsey-Boiteux rule recommends charging more products with a low price elasticity of demand, while respecting the overall constraint of covering the average cost.

A third option is to start from the average cost and add a reasonable margin so the monopoly can continue to invest - this is the *cost-plus* principle.

This cost-based regulation has been implemented since the 1950s in public companies, and it has a major drawback: since the price is set according to its costs, the monopoly has no incentive to be efficient. It will let its costs drift over time, or even overinvest, since all its investments will be reimbursed. This effect, known as the *Averch-Johnson effect*, is likely when there is an information asymmetry between the public regulator and the regulated firm. The firm knows its true costs better than the regulator and will take advantage of the situation.

To overcome this lack of incentive, the cost-based regulation could be replaced by a price-based regulation (see Laffont and Tirole, 2012) wherein the regulator sets a price cap for the monopoly. In this case, the monopoly has a strong incentive to lower its costs below the price cap in order to make a profit. The monopoly will bear any excess in costs. It is important to set the right level of this ceiling price. If the level is too high, public authorities will give up a rent to the monopoly; if it is too low, the monopoly will underinvest, which may present a risk to the quality of service.

The regulator must also define in advance a rule concerning the price cap evolution over time. For example, the $RPI - X$ rule can be used wherein the ceiling price will increase each year by the rate of inflation (Retail Price Index) minus a productivity coefficient. For instance, if inflation is 4% and the productivity coefficient is set at 1.5%, the monopoly will be authorized to increase its prices by a maximum of 2.5% from one year to the next.

In the early 1980s, this type of incentive contract was adopted in the United Kingdom during the gas deregulation and in the United States in the telecom industry, before becoming widespread in most developed countries.

Beyond its regulation, the scope of the natural monopoly is an important issue. For example, while the railway track, the signaling system, and the train stations are in a natural monopoly situation, this is not the case for the services – i.e., the transport of passengers by rail – which can be opened up to competition. We shall see in Chapter 5 how this process of gradual separation of infrastructure and service has taken place in Europe since the 1980s in most network industries such as electricity, gas, telecoms, and railways.

2. Beyond Fixed Costs: Network Effects

Economies of scale are not the only technological barrier that leads to "natural" monopoly or oligopoly situations. We can also point to network effects, which are a kind of economy of scale, but on the demand side.

There is a network effect when the utility for a user depends positively on the number of users of the same service or product. For example, a social network has a direct network effect: the more people there are on a social network ("side A" of the market in Figure 19), the more attractive it becomes for those who are already on it, insofar as the number of possible interactions increases.[13] We can also see an indirect network effect: when the number of users of a social network increases, this network becomes more attractive for advertisers, which are on the other side of the market ("side B" in Figure 19). Similarly, the more people use a search engine, the more attractive it becomes for firms that want to advertise. In some cases, there can also be a cross-network effect. Take, for example, an online hotel booking site. The more visitors there are on the platform, the more hoteliers want to be present on this platform. In return, the more hotels the platform references, the more attractive the platform becomes for consumers.

---

13   Metcalfe's law states, for example, that the utility of a network is proportional to the square of the number of its users.

Figure 19. Direct and indirect network effects

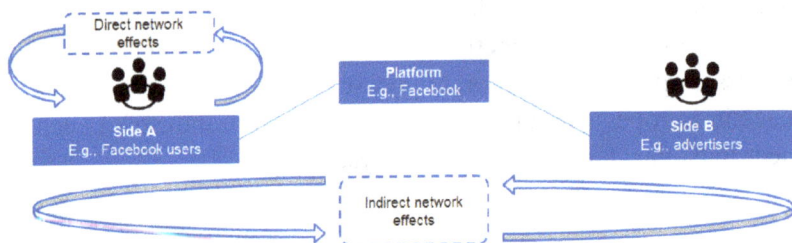

Source: DG Treasury, 2019

Network effects lead to a snowball effect, whereby one firm quickly captures all the market, and we observe a *winner-take-all* phenomenon. Competition within the market will give way to competition for the market. This process is quite similar to the one observed in a race between incompatible technological standards and can be illustrated through a simple numerical example.

Imagine two firms A and B, each offering consumers a social network service with the same quality (Table 5). The utility a consumer derives from using a social network is an increasing function of the number of users on that network. Consumers arrive in cohorts of 1,000 in each period. Since social networks A and B have the same quality (e.g., their recommendation algorithms are equally efficient), whether the first 1,000 users opt for social network A or B makes no difference. In both cases, their utility is 10. Suppose that, following an advertising campaign by social network A, the first 1,000 consumers decide to register on A. The second cohort of consumers will also choose A, but this time with full knowledge of the facts: as there are already 1,000 people connected to social network A, it is better to adopt A than B. Indeed, the utility is 12 on social network A, and only 10 on social network B since no one has signed up yet. Through a cumulative mechanism, social network A will conquer the entire market, and its performance in terms of utility will increase over time with the number of users. Social network B will never "start" the race.

Table 5. Network effect and snowball effect

Consumer cohorts	0 to 1,000	1,000 to 2,000	2,000 to 3,000	3,000 to 4,000	4,000 to 5,000
Utility for users of social network A	10	12	14	16	17
Utility for users of social network B	10	12	14	16	17

Once social network A has won the market, it becomes very difficult for a newcomer, even with better technology, to enter the market. This phenomenon, which is well known in technological standards, stems from the fact that each user has the incentive to wait for others to switch so as not to lose the existing network effect. But as consumers cannot coordinate their behavior among themselves, everyone waits, and a situation of *excess of inertia* arises: the new technology does not succeed in dethroning the old technology. We can illustrate this phenomenon with the following game theory matrix (Table 6).

Two consumers X and Y are using an old technology system (for example, a social network). This technology provides them with a utility of 5 each. If they both switch to the new technology (a new social network), their utility increases to 7, since it is of better quality. But the most damaging situation for a consumer is to be alone on a technology system, whether old or new. If this occurs, the consumer's utility is only 3. There are two Nash equilibria (defined as the best response of a consumer, given the choice of the other consumer) to this simultaneous game: (5,5) and (7,7). Since both consumers are already on the old network, it is in each consumer's interest to stay on the old network as long as the other stays. The solution of the game is (5,5), and no one switches to the new network.

Table 6. Network effect and excess inertia

	Consumer X: sticking with old technology	Consumer X: switching to new technology
Consumer Y: sticking with old technology	(5,5)	(3,3)
Consumer Y: switching to new technology	(3,3)	(7,7)

Note: The first number in each cell of the matrix corresponds to the utility withdrawn by consumer Y; the second number corresponds to the utility withdrawn by consumer X.

Network effects play a major role in digital markets today and may partly explain the high concentration of market shares.

For example, online search engines are characterized by a direct network effect: the more people use search engine X, the better the algorithm for that search engine will be, which encourages people to stay on X. Similarly, there is an indirect network effect: the more people use search engine X, the more accurate and abundant the personal data are, which will lead firms to advertise on this search engine. A snowball effect will then occur: the first users of X will give access to their personal data, which will encourage firms to advertise on search engine X. The producer of search engine X will earn revenues and invest in improving its algorithm. As the algorithm becomes more efficient, the following users will use search engine X (Figure 20).

A network effect is particularly powerful when crossed: users on side A of the market are more satisfied when there are many users on side B (and symmetrically). For example, the utility of a ride-hailing app increases for consumers with the increase in the number of drivers using the same application. Symmetrically, the utility drivers derive from using a ride-hailing app depends on the number of consumers using it.

While network effects lead to a high degree of market concentration, several factors may nevertheless favor the entry or development of new competitors:

- *Degree of product differentiation.* If products are highly differentiated, there is a space for niche operators.

- *Size of switching costs.* If switching costs are low, it is easier for a new firm to enter the market. One example is the SVOD market, where consumers can quickly and easily unsubscribe and join another firm.

- *Geographical dimension of network effects.* When network effects are essentially valued by consumers in their local dimension (such as a ride-hailing app), the cost of entry for a new operator is low.

- *Existence of markets related to the main market.* If an operator has significant market power in market A – which uses an application similar to that of market B – it will be easier for it to enter market B.

- *Multihoming.* If consumers have several applications, especially those used to compare products in terms of price or quality, it will be more difficult for a firm to conquer the entire market.

- *Constant arrival of new consumers unaffiliated with a platform and with new expectations.* For example, a young population that wants to use a different social network than their parents and with other features.

Figure 20. Network effect and quality improvement (search engine)

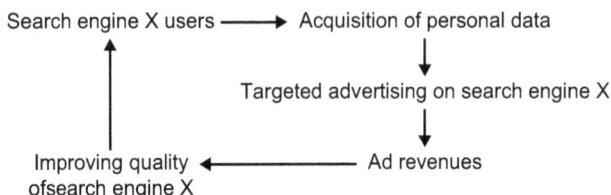

Beyond network effects, the digital economy is also characterized by high fixed costs and a marginal cost – the cost of serving an additional consumer – close to zero. For example, the fact that an additional consumer registers on a social network does not really modify the total production cost. We can deduce that the average cost decreases continuously with size; the potential market would be worldwide. We note that in April 2022, Facebook had 2.9 billion active users worldwide, or 45% of the eligible population (excluding China, which has banned Facebook).

Similarly, the digital economy is characterized by strong learning curves. A learning curve appears when the average production cost decreases with the cumulative quantity produced: the longer a firm has produced, the more experience it has accumulated in the way of producing, which lowers its average cost. In the case of digital markets, being in the market for a long time allows firms to improve algorithms and become more efficient.

Take the example of a search engine. The efficiency of an algorithm – i.e., its ability to provide a relevant answer to a user's query – improves over time, as it takes into account past search history. Similarly, in e-commerce, historical sales data can be used to improve the quality of forecasts and to continuously adjust inventory to the "right" level (Figure 21). A 2018 study by Bajari et al. on the case of Amazon shows that the quality of weekly sales forecasts on a product increases with the number of periods during which this product is offered for sale.

Figure 21. Learning curve and quality improvement (online store)

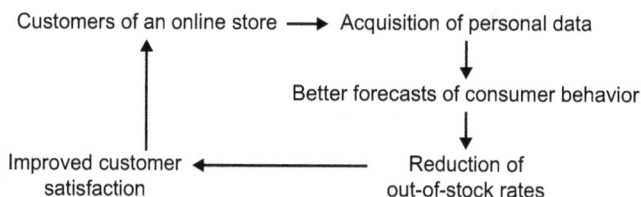

The combination of network effects, economies of scale, and learning curves logically leads to a concentration of market shares, which will persist over time. Google search thus held a market share of over 90% in Europe in 2021. In e-commerce, in 2021, Amazon represented 50% of online sales in the United States. In social networks, Facebook and Snapchat had a 90% market share in the United Kingdom in 2018 (Figure 22). To a lesser extent, similar observations can be made about platforms such as Booking, Airbnb, and Uber.

This situation of lasting concentration raises the question of platform regulation. Numerous theoretical options are possible. While cost-based tariff regulations or dismantling into several entities appear disproportionate and complex to implement, measures designed to ensure the contestability of digital markets are now attracting attention, notably through data portability (see Tirole, 2020). From this perspective, Europe proposed in 2021 to regulate large digital platforms through the Digital Markets Act (DMA) project. This *ex ante* regulation initiative aims to reinforce the contestability of digital markets, and also to instill a certain fairness, by ensuring that the practices implemented by certain digital platforms are not unfair. In addition, competition law can be a powerful tool for sanctioning potential abuses of dominance by digital players.

Figure 22. Market share of the top two operators in some digital activities (United Kingdom, 2010–2018)

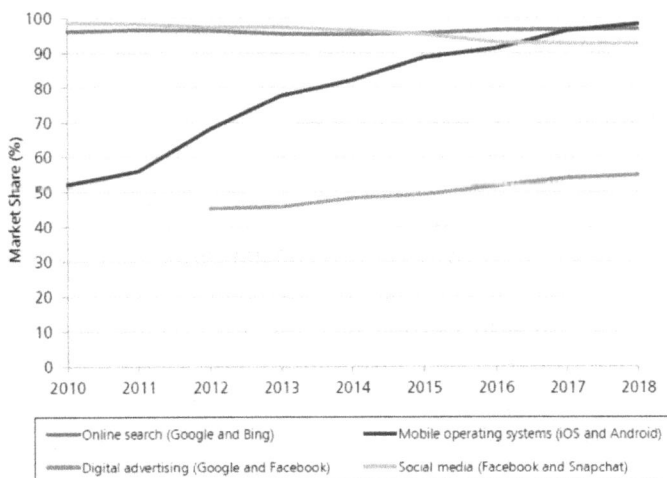

Source: Furman (2019)

II. The Role of Informational and Behavioral Barriers

Even when there are many firms in a market, competition will not be effective if there is no consumer mobility between suppliers. Search and switching costs (1) and behavioral biases (2) can hamper consumer mobility.

1. From Search Cost to Switching Costs

For competition to take place between firms, consumers must be aware of the various existing products and be able to compare them. But in reality, access to information can be costly, especially for complex products. Consumers will incur *search costs*, as highlighted by Nobel Prize winner George Stigler (1961). Firms will take advantage of these search costs to increase their prices; despite a large number of firms in the market, the intensity of competition will be altered.

For example, suppose a consumer wants to buy product X near his home. The cost of production of X is €2. Shop A sells the product down the street from his home. The consumer can also buy it in shop B. But shop B is located further from his home, and he has to bear a transport cost of €0.5. In this situation, store A can set a price higher than its production cost without fearing that the customer will go to store B: it will set a price equal to €2.49. The search cost gives firm A market power over consumers located nearby.

These search costs are not only natural costs, such as the transport cost. They can be artificially increased by firms in order to reduce competition. Firms may, for instance, create deliberately complex pricing structures, or offer differentiated packages of services to make it difficult to compare prices with those of competitors. For example, in the French mobile phone market before the entry of Free Mobile in 2012, incumbent operators proposed complex packages that included a multitude of options (quantity of SMS, unlimited numbers, time slots, and so on) and made packages difficult to compare.

What structural factors can reduce these search costs and thus increase competition?

First, the internet allows consumers to compare prices more easily. Brown and Goolsbee (2002) studied the impact of the internet on the price of life insurance contracts in the United States. They showed that the introduction of price comparison services in 1996 led to a price decrease of 8% to 15% between 1995 and 1997. This decrease is the result of the internet insofar as only the insurance contracts covered by the price comparison sites have seen their prices decrease. The authors also noted that consumers who benefited the most from the decrease in prices were those who used the internet the most. For example, life insurance contracts offered to younger consumers were priced lower than those offered to older consumers. Similarly, states where the internet was more developed experienced greater price declines.

In the same vein, Scott Morton et al. (2003) showed that search websites specializing in used cars led to a reduction in the purchase price of nearly 2% (which represents an average savings of nearly $450 per car). Most of these gains come from lower margins for dealerships receiving demands from these search websites.

Second, the presence of a well-known firm on the internet reduces search costs. Consumers will use that firm to compare prices with other suppliers. In this respect, a firm such as Amazon – which had a 50% market share in e-commerce in the United States in 2021 – has a real *benchmark* effect on the entire retail distribution sector. There is an *Amazon effect* (see Cavallo, 2018) – since consumers check the price on Amazon, competitors know that it is difficult for them to post a higher price than that of the American giant.

Beyond these search costs, competition in the market may be limited by the presence of switching costs, which represent the fixed cost consumers must bear when they want to change. These costs can have several origins (see Burnham et al., 2003):

- *Contractual exit costs.* These may include, for example, a penalty for early termination of the contract, as well as for account closure or transfer fees.

- *Time the customer will have to spend in order to know the features of the new product or service.* This is a form of learning cost, which can be high for technology products or multifunctional services (such as online banking applications).

– *Loss of loyalty capital accumulated with the former operator* (loyalty points, discount vouchers).

– *Risk of a difficult transition from the old firm to the new one, with a temporary interruption of service.* This risk can cause stress or financial penalties, similar to what can happen to a customer who changes banks and whose direct debits are not automatically transferred.

These exit costs are borne only by existing consumers, while new consumers can choose from all existing firms. This means that exit costs freeze competition more in mature markets than in emerging markets. In banking, for example, with the exception of account openings for young people, the bulk of the market is composed of previously committed consumers. We shall see in Chapter 5 how public authorities can intervene to reduce these switching costs.

2. Consumer Behavioral Biases

Even if consumers have access to all available information, it is not certain they will take advantage of competition. Consumers are subject to behavioral biases that distort their judgment and encourage them to stay loyal. Our purpose here is to provide some concrete illustrations.

A first bias is the *status quo bias*. Individuals do not like to change and prefer the situations they are already in. They therefore tend to delay choices that are nevertheless advantageous in monetary terms. For example, if a new and cheaper firm enters the market, consumers will be slow to change and will delay the termination of their contracts. For instance, very strong consumer inertia has been observed in the area of insurance contracts or savings plans.

A second behavioral bias is the *overconfidence bias*. Consumers tend to choose more expensive offers because they tend to overestimate their future consumption. For example, Malmendier and DellaVigna (2006) showed that gym users systematically overestimate their motivation to go to the gym. On the basis of registration data for gym clubs in Boston, the authors noted that consumers almost systematically make errors in their choice of membership. They often prefer a monthly fee of $70, even though they only go to the gym 4.3 times a month on average. They pay more than $17 per session, whereas they could pay $10 by buying passes by the dozen. On average, these consumers could save nearly $600 a year by paying per session rather than by the year. More than 80% of monthly subscribers make this type of consumer mistake. Rational consumers are the exception, not the norm. Similarly, in the mobile phone market, consumers tend to believe that they control their monthly usage, when in fact, many consumers regularly exceed their forecasts. Before packages became unlimited, operators may have had an incentive to price out-of-package minutes at a prohibitive price, while subsidizing the minutes included in the package.

A third behavioral bias is *myopia bias*. Consumers fail to anticipate the total cost of a product over its entire lifetime. For example, when they buy a good that requires the use of complementary goods, they will not consider the system's total price but only the price of the first good. The best-known example is that of printers and cartridges. The choice of printer should be based on the price of the cartridges. But some consumers simply compare the price of printers when making their choice. As a result, the cheapest printer may be the one that subsequently charges the most for cartridges. Improved consumer information or strong competition in the cartridge market (with the emergence of generics) can remedy this bias.

III. The Role of Strategic Barriers

Firms may engage in anti-competitive practices in order to reduce the intensity of market competition. The first practice is to collude with competitors. This is a cartel strategy (1). The second is to deter the entry of an equally effective competitor or to drive that competitor out of the market (2). The third strategy is to merge with a competitor in order to raise prices (3).

1. The Temptation to Form a Cartel

In Chapter 1, we saw that when several firms compete in the market, each exerts competitive pressure on the others, which lowers prices and profits. In these conditions, firms have a spontaneous incentive to collude in order to remove competition between them. This strategy is called a *cartel*.

A first type of cartel, which can be described as an *offensive cartel*, consists of a firm agreeing with its competitors to raise prices (Figure 23). A perfect cartel will replicate a monopoly situation. For example, suppose that two firms compete and each makes a profit of €33. In a monopoly situation, the profit would be €100. The incentive of the two firms to form a cartel is equal to: €100 − (2 × €33) = €34. By setting a monopoly price, each firm can obtain an additional €17 profit (if the extra profit is shared equally) and achieve a total profit of €50.

Figure 23. The impact of an offensive cartel on profits

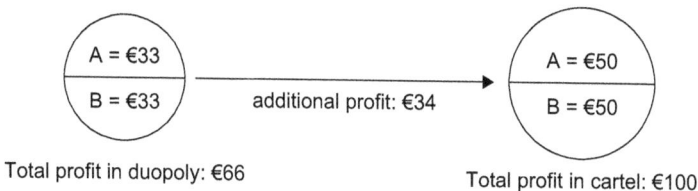

Total profit in duopoly: €66
Total profit in cartel: €100

A second type of cartel, which can be described as a *defensive cartel*, consists of planning with competitors to prevent the price from falling after the entry of a new competitor. This cartel can take the form of a collective boycott, for example, aimed at blocking the entry of a newcomer. It can also take the form of paying a competitor not to enter the market.

Suppose firm A is in a monopoly situation and is threatened by the entry of firm B. The entry will change the market from a monopoly to a duopoly situation. For example, if the monopoly profit is €100, the entry of a competitor will reduce the total profit to €66 and the profit will have to be shared by two (if both firms have the same production costs). In this case, the entry of a competitor reduces firm A's profit by €67 (€34 due to the competition effect and €33 due to the sharing of the remaining profit). In this case, firm A has a strong incentive to pay firm B not to enter. For example, if firm A offers to pay €34, this agreement is mutually beneficial. Firm B earns €1 more than if it had entered; firm A makes a profit of €66 (instead of €33 if B entered). This type of cartel was observed, for example, in the pharmaceutical sector in the United States and Europe during the 2000s. Faced with the expiry of their patents and the entry of generics, some firms "paid" the entrant in order to avoid any head-on competition.

In order to obtain a higher profit than that gained in competition, cartel members may use several methods (Table 7).

Table 7. Different cartel practices

Practice	Principle
Price fixing	Firms agree directly on a given price or a price increase, or on a common formula to calculate the price.
Market or customer allocation	Firms divide markets geographically or per customer.
Bid rigging in calls for tender	During a call for tender, firms designate in advance the winner but submit "fake" bids, to give the appearance of competing against each other.
Quotas	Firms collectively decide to reduce production in order to raise prices; they allocate quotas, based on the marginal production costs of each firm.
Collective boycott	Firms agree to prevent a competitor from entering the market, principally by colluding with suppliers upstream.

Statistical studies show that cartels tend to develop in markets with a small number of suppliers (oligopoly) or a concentrated supply. Moreover, they often concern intermediate products. Combe and Monnier (2012) showed that over two thirds of the cartels detected in Europe occurred in sectors such as metallurgy, chemicals, machinery and equipment manufacturing, or materials. Strong barriers to entry and exit (of a legal or economic nature) favor the development of cartels.

Insofar as cartels are only intended to reduce competition, they are economically inefficient. They lead to artificial price increases, without any counterpart for the consumers, who buy the same products as before but at a higher price. The 2015 empirical study of Boyer and Kotchoni on a large sample of 1,119 cartels showed that the price increases resulting from a cartel were quite significant: the overcharge was between 13% and 17% (Table 8).

Table 8. Estimates of cartel overcharges in Europe and the United States

		All Cartels	OE > 0%	0%<OE≤49%	OE>49%	Cartels Before 1973	Cartels After 1973
All locations	Mean	15.47	16.68	16.47	17.31	13.97	16.07
	Median	16.01	16.17	16.17	16.48	14.18	16.41
	prop.	100.00	92.77	69.88	22.87	28.51	71.49
US	Mean	14.36	15.82	15.69	16.30	15.13	14.00
	Median	14.48	15.19	15.04	16.13	16.37	14.20
	prop.	30.02	27.25	21.36	5.90	9.65	20.37
EU	Mean	13.51	14.43	14.05	15.39	12.54	14.15
	Median	14.08	14.20	13.67	15.32	13.18	15.86
	prop.	33.51	31.36	22.52	8.85	13.40	20.11
Domestic	Mean	12.93	14.21	14.09	14.86	13.08	12.87
	Median	13.68	13.81	13.79	14.09	13.39	13.81
	prop.	46.82	42.62	36.01	6.61	14.47	32.35
International	Mean	17.71	18.78	19.01	18.30	14.89	18.71
	Median	18.66	19.29	19.38	18.26	15.34	20.66
	prop.	53.17	50.13	33.87	16.26	14.03	39.14

Source: Boyer and Kotchoni (2015)

As in the case of a monopoly (see Chapter 1), cartels also lead to a welfare loss, as some consumers will not buy the product because of its higher price. Beyond this static inefficiency, cartels can also generate dynamic inefficiency: as competition no longer constrains firms, their incentive to innovate and lower their costs is reduced. As a result, the society is deprived of efficiencies that would have been developed if firms had had to compete.

As we will see in Chapter 6, cartels are prohibited by antitrust laws, and the penalties imposed can be significant.

2. The Use of Deterrence Strategies

A firm with a monopoly position may have the incentive to implement an entry deterrence strategy.

Suppose that firm A is in a monopolistic situation; it makes a profit of €100 each period (Figure 24). If competitor B enters the market, both firms are in a Cournot duopoly situation, and the total profit, which must be shared between firms A and B, will decrease to €66. Firm A has an incentive to spend up to €67 to deter B from entering the market; without the threat of entry, firm A would not have incurred such an expense.

Figure 24. The impact of competitor B's entry on firm A's profits

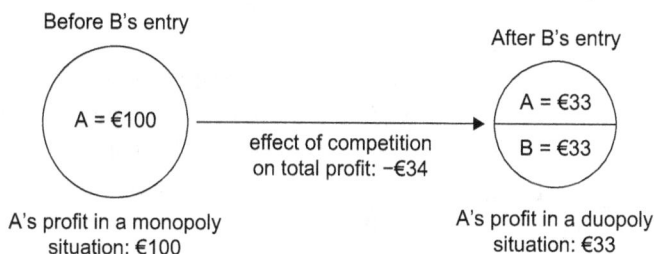

Before B's entry

A = €100

effect of competition on total profit: −€34

After B's entry

A = €33

B = €33

A's profit in a monopoly situation: €100

A's profit in a duopoly situation: €33

Since the 1960s, an abundant economic literature has developed on the entry deterrence strategy. It appears that two main conditions must be met:

- *Deterrence must be relatively inexpensive.* Indeed, if the cost of deterrence is prohibitive compared to the gain it provides, it is better to let the new competitor enter. In our numerical example, if deterrence costs €68, it is better for firm A to do nothing.

- *Deterrence must be credible.* The monopoly must do more than simply threaten the newcomer. It must incur an irreversible investment to prove its determination to deter entry. For example, when a drug patent is about to expire, a firm may decide to preemptively launch its own generic (i.e., before its own patent expires) to take the wind out of the sails of the generics.

While theoretically possible, this deterrence strategy is very difficult to demonstrate empirically since the potential competitor has not entered the market. Moreover, a strategy of entry deterrence is ambivalent for consumers. If we take the example of the patent holder launching its own generics before patent expiration, these generics enable patients to have a cheaper generic version before the patent expires. On the other hand, the patent holder's own generics may limit competition from independent generics after the patent has expired.

A second, more easily detected anticompetitive strategy is to exclude an equally efficient competitor – a practice of exclusion (Figure 25). Let's assume that firm A is dominant in the market with a 75% market share and makes a profit of €45. It faces a small competitor B, which has a 25% market share and makes a profit of €15. If firm A succeeds in "pushing" its competitor out of the market, it will not only recover B's market share and its profit of €15, but also find itself in a monopoly position with an additional profit of €40. The incentive for firm A to exclude firm B from the market is therefore very strong. It is equal to the difference between the monopoly profit and its duopoly profit, i.e., €55.

Figure 25. The aim of an exclusionary strategy

Situation before the exclusion of B from the market

Profit of A €45

Profit of B €15

Additional profit: €40

Situation after the exclusion of B from the market

Profit of A €100

In order to exclude its competitor, the dominant firm may use different methods such as tying,[14] loyalty discounts, exclusivity agreements with consumers, refusal of access to essential infrastructure, disparagement,

---

14   Tied selling is the sales of several different products at the same time.

or predatory pricing. We will see in Chapter 6 how the competition authorities sanction this type of practice, qualified as *abuse of dominant position.*

3. The Impact of Mergers on Competition

A third strategy for reducing competition is to buy out competitors.

For example, if the market is initially a duopoly, a merger will lead to a monopoly situation. In the case of Ryanair's proposed takeover of Aer Lingus in 2007, the Commission found that the new entity would have a monopoly on 22 routes from Dublin, which would have led to increases in ticket prices.

But as a rule, a merger does not put an end to all effective competition in the market, insofar as it does not involve all the firms; mergers are most often between two operators in oligopolistic markets. In this case, the final impact of the merger on prices will depend crucially on the reaction of firms not involved in the merger (known as *outsiders*).

First, a merger between competitors may lead to higher prices through a so-called *unilateral effect*: as there is less competitive pressure in the market, prices will rise. More precisely, if we take the case of a Cournot oligopoly, the merging firms (*insiders*) will reduce their output, while firms outside the merger (*outsiders*) will react by increasing their output, but to a lesser extent – leading to a price increase.

We can illustrate this phenomenon with an example. Let's assume three symmetrical firms A, B, C in a Cournot competition. Before the merger, each firm makes a profit of €8 (Figure 26) and the total profit is €24. Firm A decides to buy out competitor B; the market share of the new entity (A + B) rises to 66%, and the market becomes a duopoly, with less competitive pressure. By acquiring firm B, firm A not only recovers B's market share and profit (equal to €8), but also benefits from a reduction in competition since there are now only two firms in the market. The total profit increases from €24 to €30. The total gain from the merger for firms A and B is therefore (€20 − €16) = €4. It should be noted that firm C, which remains outside the merger, also benefits from this reduction in competition (in the absence of efficiency gains): its profit increases by (€10 − €8), or €2.

Figure 26. The impact of a merger on profits (in Cournot)

Profits before the merger · · · · · · · · · · · · · · Profits after the merger

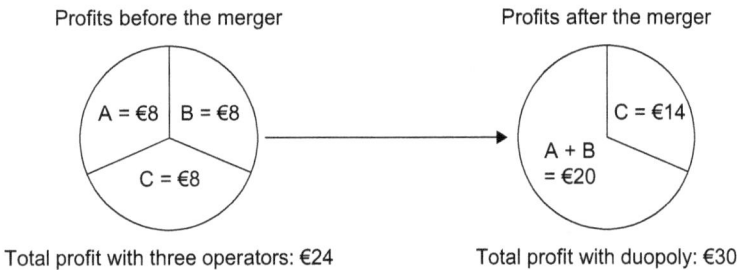

A = €8 | B = €8

C = €8

C = €14

A + B = €20

Total profit with three operators: €24 · · · · · · · · Total profit with duopoly: €30

Second, a merger between competitors may lead to a price increase through another mechanism, known as the *coordinated effect*: the new market structure may facilitate tacit collusion between firms. In the case of a Cournot oligopoly, this means that outsiders react by also reducing their output. This coordinated effect results from the mere oligopolistic interaction of firms and the understanding of a common line of action, without the need for explicit coordination as in the case of a cartel.

One can even go further and consider that the purpose of a merger may not be to reduce existing competition but to prevent the development of future competition.

This preemption risk can be illustrated by an example. Let's assume that firm A is in a monopoly position and makes a profit of €100. Firm B has developed a competing product Y and plans to enter the market.

If firm A does not react, the market situation will evolve into a duopoly, with total profits falling from €100 to €66, divided equally between the two firms. In order to avoid the entry of firm B, firm A has a strong incentive to buy it out – A is willing to spend the difference between the monopoly profit and its duopoly profit, i.e., (€100 – €33) = €67. The purpose of buying B is to prevent the entry of a competitor into the market. Sometimes described as a *killer acquisition*, this type of strategy is difficult to detect by antitrust authorities, even though these practices have been highlighted in the pharmaceutical industry. For example, Cunningham et al. (2018) showed that 6% of acquisitions in this sector have the effect of stopping the acquired firm's R&D efforts on projects competing with those carried out by the acquiring firm.

Chapter 5

Policies to Strengthen Competition

Competition intensity in a market is influenced not only by economic and technological characteristics, but also by the legal environment. In other words, public authorities govern competition through regulations that affect the conditions for firms to enter and operate in the market.

In order to increase the intensity of competition, public authorities can use four main levers (Table 9):

- Facilitate consumer mobility by improving transparency of information and reducing switching costs.

- Encourage the entry of new firms by lowering regulatory barriers.

- Increase the country's openness to imports by lowering trade barriers.

- Deregulate access to services in network industries.

We will take up these different economic policy levers in turn, high-lighting the political obstacles to their implementation.

Table 9. The four main levers to strengthen competition

Public policy objective	Main levers
Strengthening consumer mobility between suppliers	• Better consumer information on prices and product features. • Measures to reduce switching costs.
Alleviating/updating sectoral rules	• Increase in the numerus clausus and authorization thresholds. • Entry of new operators.
Lowering the price of imported products	• Reduction of tariffs and non-tariff barriers.
Ending the monopoly situation in network industries	• Separation of the infrastructure and the service. • Regulation of the infrastructure access. • Opening up to competition for the market (through tendering) or in the market (through the entry of new firms).

I. Strengthening Consumer Information and Mobility

A first lever for public action is to foster consumer mobility by providing better information on prices and product characteristics, and by promoting mobility between suppliers.

1. Acting on the Transparency of Information

As we saw in Chapter 4, consumers are able to switch if they are informed of what they are actually paying, and if they know the existence of alternative opportunities. However, the presence of search costs limits their incentive to compare products and prices.

A first lever of public action consists of reinforcing the quality of information available to consumers, in particular in activities like banking. In France, for example, the 2008 Chatel Act introduced an annual statement of bank charges. At the beginning of the year, banks must send each customer a document summarizing the total charges paid in the previous year. This statement includes, for example, the interest earned on a debit position on the account (agios). Since 2011, banks have been required to indicate on the customer's monthly account statement all bank charges that have been applied. These measures provide consumers with clearer information on the cost of their banking services.

A second lever for public action consists of setting up a public price comparator. Such a system exists in France for fuels. All consumers are informed in real time of the prices of all gas stations in the country. A public price comparator has the advantage of being neutral, which is not always the case with private comparators, and it is based on a transparent data collection methodology. However, generalizing price comparators to all sectors is difficult, because products are often heterogeneous.

A third lever of public action consists of requiring suppliers to display all their prices on their websites, including products not sold online. The Israeli government implemented this type of public policy in 2015. Ater and Rigbi (2017) studied the competitive impact of this measure, comparing price levels before and after the law came into force. To be sure that the effect on prices resulted from the increased transparency and not from other factors, the authors took two control groups (Figure 27):

- Products that were already sold online before the introduction of the law (group 1).

- Products whose prices were widely known to consumers (group 2).

The most immediate effect of the mandatory display of prices on the internet was to reduce price dispersion for the same product: the same product, which previously had 16 different prices on average in Israel, now only has five. The price dispersion observed in the stores now subject to this law (yellow curve in Figure 27) is quite similar to that observed in the two control groups (green and blue curves in Figure 27).

Figure 27. Impact of price display on price dispersion

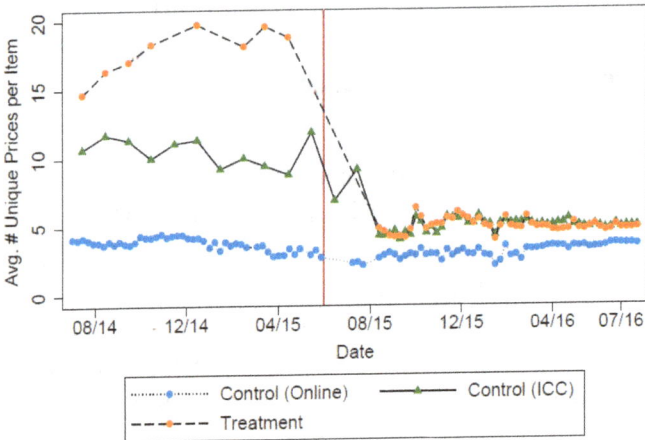

Source: Ater and Rigbi (2017)

Moreover, the transparency of information gradually reduced the prices by an average of 4% to 5% compared to the two control groups. According to the authors, this decrease can be explained by the frequent use of price comparators, but also by the fact that the media widely communicated on this new legislation. However, the decrease in prices appears to be quite differentiated according to brands and products:

- It is strong for supermarket chains with a high pricing policy; conversely, the price drop is not observed in hard discount chains, whose prices were already low.

- It is not visible for stores that were already subject to strong local competition.

– It has mostly affected the main brand products sold in all stores.

The imposition of a price display on the internet will not always lower prices. Price transparency can also encourage, in specific cases, tacit collusion between firms, leading to higher prices. For example, the Chilean government made it mandatory in 2012 to display the fuel price in real time on the internet. Luco (2019) showed that this decision led to an increase in distributor margins by 9%. The main reason is that the oligopolistic structure of the market favored information exchange between a small number of firms, which led to price coordination.

2. The Reduction of Transfer Costs

Access to better information is a necessary but insufficient condition for consumers to switch. As discussed in Chapter 3, competition may also be limited by switching costs for already committed consumers. Switching costs are not always unjustified if they result, for example, from an investment relationship between a firm and its customers. The firm offers customers advantageous terms when they arrive but imposes exit costs in return. For example, in the French mobile phone industry, the phone subsidy offered by firms implies that customers commit to a certain duration (12 or 24 months). If they cancel their contract before the end of the term, they must pay a penalty. This model is economically justified; the firm loses money in the short term by subsidizing the phone, and then makes money during the term of the contract.

Therefore, the regulation of exit costs should not lead to their elimination, but rather to the reduction of those that are not justified or proportionate. The main public levers include:

– *Clear information on the amount of exit penalties.* For example, in France, banks are required to inform new account openers how much it will cost to transfer their assets to another bank. This approach complements the bank mobility assistance, which is provided at the time of departure.

– *Facilitated portability.* Public authorities can encourage the transfer from one operator to another. For example, in the French mobile phone sector, the Chatel Act introduced online telephone number portability within 24 hours in 2008. In banking, one measure to facilitate mobility is to simplify the procedures for changing banks. In France, the Macron Act (2015) introduced the "bank mandate," which exempts the customer from notifying the issuers of direct debits.

– *Minimum standardization of tariffs.* In sectors such as retail banking or mobile phones, the differentiation of products between operators makes it difficult to compare offers. To deal with this problem, public authorities can encourage firms to standardize part of their offer – for example, according to typical consumer profiles. They can also encourage firms to offer, in addition to their own product range, a common platform of basic services. This allows all consumers to compare the prices of simple and identical packages.

II. Reducing Regulatory Barriers

Market entry, particularly in service activities, is often governed by regulatory barriers, which take different forms that are more or less restrictive:

– Requirement to register with a government agency before practicing

- Certification that allows firms to practice as long as they meet a certain number of criteria

- Professional licensing, which is a "right to practice" – in the U.S. case, Kleiner and Krueger (2010) found that the percentage of workers who require a license to practice has risen from 5% in the early 1950s to 29% in 2006

- Regulation of the number of operators in the market through a numerus clausus

- Regulation of firms' characteristics, leading, for example, to the prohibition of certain business models (such as the sale of medicines in supermarkets).

Once in the market, there are also rules relating to "good practices," which may be laid down in codes of ethics.

The extent of these different regulatory barriers can be measured through the OECD's Product Market Regulation (PMR) indicator. This composite indicator assigns each country a score on a scale from 0 (no access restrictions) to 6 (high access restrictions). In 2018, OECD countries had an average score of 1.38 out of 6, meaning most markets were fairly open (beyond the minimum rules for safety or public health purposes).

In France, for instance (Figure 28), the indicator is slightly above average (1.57/6), especially in an activity like pharmaceutical distribution. In this respect, the OECD (2019a) underlines the sectoral barriers that limit the entry of new firms, particularly in services:

As regards the services of notaries, architects, accountants, real estate agents, and lawyers, France continues to have some of the highest barriers to entry and practice controls in the OECD area . . . . For example, the regulatory framework governing accounting services also requires that audit firms be owned by licensed auditors; similarly, the majority of shares in architectural services firms must be owned by licensed architects. . . . France is the country with the most restrictive regulations for the retail sale of medicines. Pharmacies continue to have a monopoly on the sale of basic medicines and are subject to significant restrictions on ownership and size, capital, distribution chains, and online sales. In addition, taxi and chauffeur-driven car (VTC) drivers are required to hold specific qualifications in order to carry passengers, which are not justified by safety considerations.

Figure 28. Regulations for certain services in France

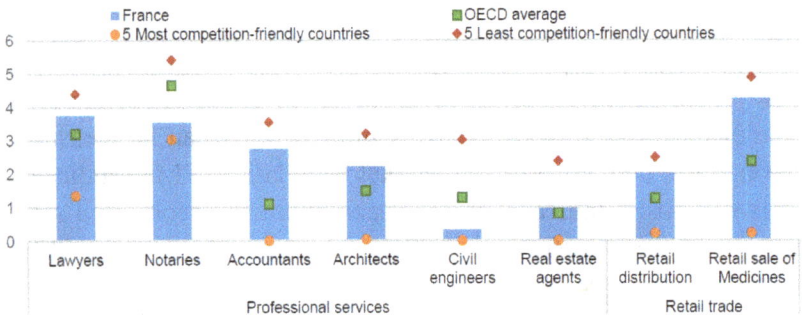

Source: OECD (2019a)

A second indicator to assess the extent of entry restrictions is the "Occupational Entry Regulation" indicator (see OECD, 2020), which focuses more specifically on access to professions in the services sector. It also results in a score between 0 (no regulation at all) and 6 (highly regulated activity). There is a high degree of heterogeneity in the levels of regulation between countries, and sometimes high levels, as in South Africa (see Figure 29). In the United States, more than 1,100 professions require a license in at least one of the American states (see Kleiner and Krueger, 2010).

Figure 29. Restrictions on access to an occupation in services

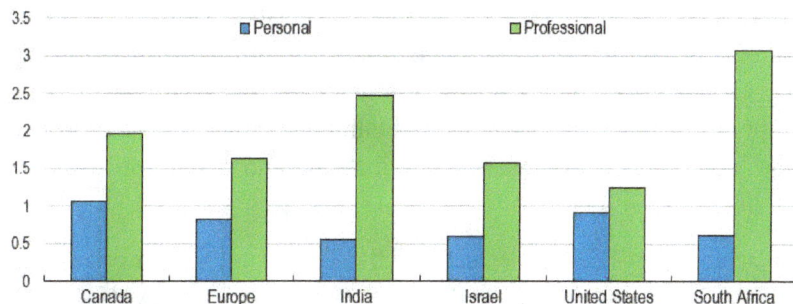

Source: OECD (2020)

1. Regulatory Barriers as an Obstacle to Competition

Are these regulatory barriers justified? Economic theory provides a nuanced answer to this question.

According to a first approach, these barriers are intended to ensure a minimum quality. In fact, the provision of services is characterized by a strong asymmetry of information between suppliers and consumers – it is difficult for the customer to know whether the service provided is of good quality or whether it is necessary. This is particularly true for *credence goods* such as car repairs. Even after the service has been provided, the customer is unable to know whether the repair was justified or proportionate. In the absence of any regulation, there is a risk that poor-quality firms will drive out good-quality firms by charging low prices in return for poor-quality service. To prevent this risk, public authorities can set up a selection system at entry, ensuring that suppliers have the minimum qualifications and the appropriate probity. While this results in a reduction in competition, this negative effect is counterbalanced by an increase in the average quality of service.

However, a second, more liberal approach considers these barriers to entry as the expression of private interests – namely, those of incumbent firms. Their objective is to limit entry (for example, by introducing a numerus clausus or a licensing system) with the sole aim of reducing competition and obtaining an artificial *scarcity rent*. The legal barrier then becomes unjustified and disproportionate to the objective of quality.

What are the observed effects of these restrictions on economic activity? Empirical studies fail to show that a high level of legal barriers has a positive effect on service quality (see Bambalaite et al., 2020). In particular, with the rise of digital technology, strong *ex ante* regulation becomes less necessary, as there is now *ex post* regulation through rating systems – a poor-quality supplier will be rated poorly by consumers and will be gradually driven out of the market (see Farronato et al., 2020).

Conversely, empirical studies comparing countries with different levels of regulation for identical occupations highlight that over-regulation of entry has a negative effect on the level of employment, prices, and productivity. In particular, the negative effect on productivity goes through two main channels (see Bambalaite et al., 2020):

- Barriers protect incumbent firms from newcomers, reducing their incentive to innovate and improve service quality.

- Barriers restrict the growth of the most efficient firms in the market, because regulations limit labor mobility within and between sectors. In particular, since regulations differ from country to country, they impede the labor's geographical mobility.

The regulation of retail trade in France during the period 1973–2005 is a good illustration of the undesirable effects of excessive regulation. The aim of the French government was to preserve small businesses from large-scale distribution and to control commercial urban planning. A first series of measures enacted by the Royer (1973)[15] and Raffarin (1996) laws[16] consisted of lowering the threshold for authorizing the opening of a new shop from 1,500 square meters to 300 square meters. Beyond 300 square meters, authorization became necessary from 1996 onwards, granted by a local commission on which the competitors sat. A second type of restriction concerned the threshold of resale at a loss: the Galland Act (1996)[17] defined it restrictively, without including "backward margins." Thus, a product bought from a producer at €10 had to be resold at least at €10, even when the distributor had received subsequent discounts from the producer.

These various restrictions have resulted in a strong local concentration of retailers in favor of incumbent retailers, and an inflationary drift in food products in the 2000s, while the result on employment has been negative. These regulations have not prevented the decline of small independent shops. Thus, Bertrand and Kramarz (2002) showed that the Royer law limited the entry of new retailers insofar as these retailers had to obtain authorization from a local commission. It appears that the localities where the restrictions on entry were the strongest were also those where job creation in the retail sector was the lowest. In other words, when local boards prevented the entry of a new retail outlet, employment was penalized. The authors estimated that if no permission had been granted, retail employment would have been 7% to 15% higher, or between 112,000 and 240,000 additional jobs. In the same vein, Askenazy and Weidenfeld (2007) showed that the Raffarin law prevented the creation of 50,000 to 100,000 net jobs by restricting the entry of new competitors into the market.[18]

---

15   Law no. 73-1193 of 27 December 1973.

16   Law no. 96-603 of 5 July 1996.

17   Law no. 96-588 of 1 July 1996.

18   In view of these undesirable effects, the regulation of commercial planning evolved between 2005 and 2008 in the direction of partial liberalization.

2. Political Obstacles to Sectoral Deregulation

Given the undesirable impacts of excessive regulation on employment, prices, and productivity, public authorities should reduce regulatory barriers when they appear excessive and unjustified. For example, in the case of France, many reports have called for a reform of the "regulated" professions, such as the Armand-Rueff (1959), Cahuc-Kramarz (2004), and Attali (2008) reports.

These regulatory reforms could have strong and positive effects on productivity gains. Cette et al. (2018) estimated the productivity gains that would result from reforms leading to the reduction of artificial barriers. They distinguished between regulations related to state intervention in the market and those related to state-introduced entry barriers. They also took into account the fact that regulations create rents that can be shared between firms and their employees. Their result is instructive: the largest overall impact would be in Italy and France (5.7% and 5.4%, respectively), followed by Austria, Spain, and Canada (over 4%). These countries have the highest levels of entry regulation. The impact on productivity is lower in Sweden, Australia, and the United Kingdom (less than 2%), followed by the Netherlands (2.3%) – the least regulated countries. These simulations confirm that the expected gains from implementing ambitious product market reforms could be significant – around 3.6% on average in OECD countries.

These reforms would have a direct (but not necessarily immediate) effect not only on consumers and their purchasing power, but also on the competitiveness of firms that use these services. For example, Barone and Cingano (2011) analyzed the effects of increased competition in energy, transportation services, communication services, and professional services on the GDP, productivity, and exports in the manufacturing sectors over the period spanning from 1996 to 2002.

The authors found that if the more restrictive countries aligned their regulations with those of the more flexible countries, they experienced higher growth, labor productivity, and exports. The barriers were mainly found in the regulation of energy and professional services. Concerning the latter, the authors showed that removing restrictions on comparative advertising and pricing freedom would increase growth by 0.5% in the industries most dependent on professional services.

While reforms to lower sectoral barriers can have positive effects on the economy, they are difficult to implement because there is a strong asymmetry between the winners and losers of such reforms. Indeed, any sectoral liberalization has redistributive effects. On the winning side, new entrants and consumers see prices fall, quality improves, and market access facilitated. On the losing side, incumbents and their employees see their margins or remuneration fall (Cahuc et al., 2006. The problem is that policy-makers and public opinion do not perceive the gains and losses resulting from increased competition symmetrically.

The gains from increased competition are often underestimated. This is because new entrants are not yet present in the market and therefore cannot demonstrate the beneficial effects of their entry, particularly in terms of job creation or purchasing power. Moreover, new entrants have little access to political power and public decision-making, as they do not yet have sufficient visibility. As for consumers, they are not necessarily aware of the total amount of gains resulting from increased competition since these gains are spread over a very large number of consumers. For example, in the case of Free Mobile's entry in France, the gain for a person who already had a mobile phone subscription in 2012 was around €5 per month, or €60 per year. This sum appears to be quite limited at the individual level; but at the aggregate level, the annual gain in purchasing power is €3.3 billion. Moreover, consumers do not constitute an organized group capable of influencing political decisions because there are too many. This is the *Olson paradox* of collective action; the more members a group has, the less able it is to organize itself, because each individual lets others act. As a result, the voices of consumers and new entrants are rarely represented at the political level.

On the losing side, we find incumbent firms that will be negatively affected (at least in the short term) by increased competition. Indeed, as soon as entry is restricted by legal barriers, a "scarcity rent" arises, reflecting scarcity of supply relative to demand. Increased competition will therefore reduce the value of this rent. For example, the price of a taxi medallion (known as a *license*) in Paris, which had reached €230,000 in 2013, fell to €125,000 in 2017 – a 45% drop. This very sharp fall in value is largely explained by the arrival of ride-hailing services.

It is therefore quite logical that incumbents will mobilize against pro-competitive reforms. Their political clout and influence are significant, as they are well known by government and media. They also have a more detailed knowledge of the political decision-making process. In particular cases, there may be a phenomenon of *regulator capture*: the proximity with public authorities is such that the authorities become the spokesperson for the incumbent firms' particular interests. In particular, if the market is open to competition, incumbent firms can invoke the risk of redundancies or bankruptcy, with its dramatic social consequences at the local level. When they are few, the *insiders* can organize collective action; the Olson paradox states that small groups take action more often insofar as the non-participation of one of their members exerts a strong impact on the final result. Incumbent firms will mobilize and make their voices heard, also involving employees and their trade union representatives. They will ask public authorities for restrictive regulations in order to block the entry of new competitors, or they will rely on a complication of the existing rules to make entry more expensive. According to the public choice theory, regulation is then motivated more by insiders' private interests than by the general interest.

Incumbent firms, when they benefit from a scarcity rent, may share it with employees, which further complicates the implementation of a pro-competitive reform. In the case of France, Cette et al. (2018) highlight that state-installed barriers to entry create rent, part of which is appropriated by workers through higher wages.

Given this asymmetry of forces, pro-competitive reforms are difficult to implement and receive little public support.

When pro-competitive reforms are nevertheless adopted, they often take the form of a policy of very gradual "small steps". The aim is to make the reform politically acceptable to the incumbents by smoothing its effects over time. For example, the entry of new notaries was encouraged by the Macron law (2015)[19] but this law did not introduce a regime of total freedom. Instead, it implemented the gradual increase of the number of notaries on the basis of geographical zoning, authorizing the creation of new offices.

One option to make pro-competitive reforms more politically acceptable would be to compensate the losers, i.e., the incumbents. For example, in the case of taxis, the value of the license was negatively impacted by the growth of ride-hailing services from 2011. The state could compensate taxi drivers for the decrease in their license price.[20] But this solution would be particularly costly for public finances: delpla and Wyplosz (2007) estimated that, for France, the purchase of taxi licenses would cost €4.5 billion.

---

19   Law no. 2015-990 of 6 August 2015. For a first assessment of its impact, one can read the note of the Commission for the Study of the Effects of the Law for Growth and Activity (2017): https://www.strategie. gouv.fr/sites/strategie.gouv.fr/files/atoms/files/fiche-professions_0.pdf

20   Another option is to give all license holders a second license free of charge, thereby limiting the loss of value of their assets while increasing the supply of taxis.

III. Opening Up to Imports

In order to strengthen competition in the domestic market, public authorities can increase the country's openness to imports by lowering tariff and non-tariff barriers. Protectionism reduces internal competition, which is costly for consumers – but also in terms of cost per job saved (1.). A reduction in protectionism will exert competitive pressure on domestic producers. They will react by lowering their prices and increasing their productivity. However, strong political obstacles make it difficult to implement a policy of trade liberalization (2.).

1. Protectionism as a Restriction of Competition

Protectionism consists of setting up tariff or non-tariff barriers (such as quotas) with the aim of limiting imports in the domestic market. These policies will increase domestic production and local employment.

Economic theory shows that, as a general rule, protectionism is a costly policy for society. Indeed, when a country introduces a customs duty on an imported good, the mechanical effect is to raise prices in the domestic market: domestic producers, now protected from foreign competition, will adjust their prices upwards. Their profits will increase. Consumers, on the other hand, suffer a loss of purchasing power because the price has increased. In addition, some consumers give up buying the product because of the price increase. It can be shown that the overall effect of protectionism on welfare is negative insofar as the loss of consumer surplus is not compensated by the increase in profits.

However, if protectionism penalizes consumers, it saves jobs in return: the welfare losses must be balanced with the jobs saved. This reasoning is correct in principle and must therefore be assessed empirically. At what cost does protectionism succeed in saving jobs?

An empirical study by the Dallas Federal Reserve (2002) on the 20 most protected sectors in the United States showed that the annual cost of protectionism for consumers amounted to $44 billion; in return, it saved 191,764 jobs, making the cost per job saved $231,289 (Table 10). More recently, Flaaen et al. (2019a) analyzed the effect of the 2018 taxes that Donald Trump imposed on washing machines imported from Asia. Their main result is that the price of washing machines increased by 12% in the United States, leading to a tax on U.S. consumers of $1.5 billion in 2018. The protectionist measures in turn saved 1,800 jobs, making the annual cost per job saved more than $800,000. What these studies show is that protectionism does save jobs, but at a huge cost to society.

Table 10. The cost per job saved from protectionism in the United States

	Protected industry	Jobs saved	Total cost (in millions)	Annual cost per job saved
1	Benzenoid chemicals	216	$ 297	$ 1,376,435
2	Luggage	226	290	1,285,078
3	Softwood lumber	605	632	1,044,271
4	Sugar	2,261	1,868	826,104
5	Polyethylene resins	298	242	812,928
6	Dairy products	2,378	1,630	685,323
7	Frozen concentrated orange juice	609	387	635,103
8	Ball bearings	146	88	603,368
9	Maritime services	4,411	2,522	571,668
10	Ceramic tiles	347	191	551,367
11	Machine tools	1,556	746	479,452
12	Ceramic articles	418	140	335,876
13	Women's handbags	773	204	263,535
14	Canned tuna	390	100	257,640
15	Glassware	1,477	366	247,889
16	Apparel and textiles	168,786	33,629	199,241
17	Peanuts	397	74	187,223
18	Rubber footwear	1,701	286	168,312
19	Women's nonathletic footwear	3,702	518	139,800
20	Costume jewelry	1,067	142	132,870
	Total **Average (weighted)**	**191,764**	**$44,352**	$ **231,289**

Source: Dallas Federal Reserve (2002)

This high cost per job saved is confirmed if we take into account that protectionism in one sector can have a negative effect on employment in other sectors. For example, if the sugar sector is protected, this increases not only the price of sugar but also the price of products that use sugar as an ingredient, such as confectionery. The price increase of confectionery will lead consumers to buy less, forcing manufacturers to lay off workers. The jobs saved in sugar production, thanks to protectionism, will be balanced with jobs destroyed downstream. In a study on the tire sector, Hufbauer and Lowry (2012) estimated that Barack Obama's protectionist measures against Chinese imports have saved 1,200 jobs, at a total cost of $1.1 billion, i.e., a cost per job saved of $900,000. In addition, the extra cost paid by consumers led them to reduce their spending in the retail sector, resulting in the loss of 3,731 jobs in this sector. The net job bill for the U.S. economy is negative, amounting to $3,731 - 1,200 = 2,531$ jobs … lost.

Similarly, the cost per job saved does not take into account the fact that other countries will retaliate. They will in turn tax imports from the country that has protected itself. A Federal Reserve study by Flaaen and Pierce (2019b) measured the overall employment impact of protectionism implemented since 2018 by Donald Trump, taking into account this indirect effect. In response to U.S. protectionism, the Chinese have adopted retaliatory measures. As a result, the exports of American firms to China have shrunk, reducing the number of jobs. This negative effect on employment, estimated at −0.7%, leads to a final negative employment balance of −1.5%.

2. Obstacles to Opening Up to Imports

In view of the above results, a policy of trade liberalization, consisting of lowering protectionist barriers, would increase collective welfare; the threat of imports would stimulate competition in the domestic market, forcing producers to lower their prices.

In the American case, Jaravel and Sager (2019) measured the impact of opening up to Chinese imports on consumer prices, and they found a strong effect – a 1% increase in the penetration rate of Chinese imports results in a drop in prices of around 2%. This effect is mainly due to increased competition, which forces U.S. producers to adjust their prices downwards. When the Chinese import penetration rate increases by 1%, the margin rate of domestic firms decreases by 1.75%. This margin effect is particularly important in markets where domestic industrial concentration is initially high: here, Chinese imports impose a competitive discipline. The annual purchasing power of each American household has increased by $1,500 over the period spanning from 2000 to 2007. This effect is particularly significant for low-income households, whose purchasing power has increased by 15% over the average, given the characteristics of imported products (low-end textile clothing, and so on).

This pro-competitive impact of international trade can be illustrated by a simple example (Figure 30).

Suppose two autarkic countries X and Y. In each country, there is a flour producer (producer A and producer B, respectively) in a monopoly situation. We assume that the flour is exactly the same in both countries. Before the opening to trade, each producer charges a monopoly price on its domestic market and obtains a profit of €100. Countries A and B decide to open up to trade with each other. The two domestic markets will move from two national monopolies to a Cournot duopoly. Indeed, in each country, the domestic producer is now confronted with the imports of its foreign competitor. Each firm will conquer half of its rival's market, lowering the flour price in both countries. The total profit of each firm will evolve from €100 to (2 × €33), or €66. The gain of this international opening for consumers is the result of a pure competition effect: the passage from a monopoly to a duopoly situation has decreased the rent of domestic producers. We can see here that international trade of identical goods (*intra-industry trade*) brings a gain for consumers in both countries – by way of lower prices – through a competitive effect.

Figure 30. The effect of opening up to trade

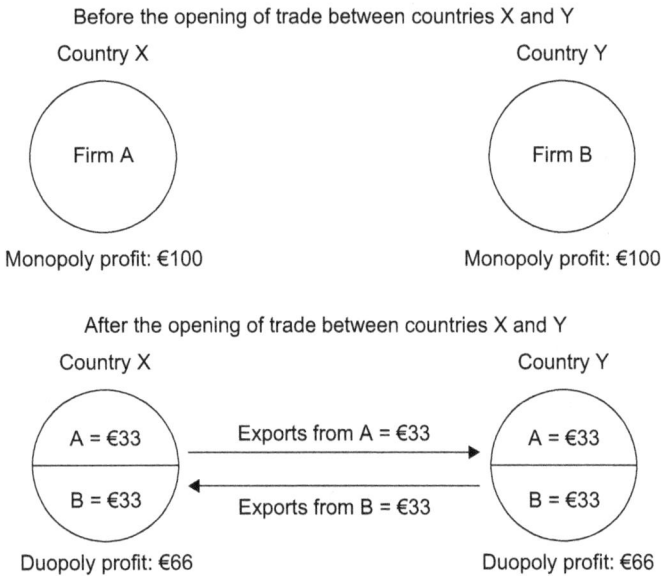

Before the opening of trade between countries X and Y

Country X   Country Y

Firm A   Firm B

Monopoly profit: €100   Monopoly profit: €100

After the opening of trade between countries X and Y

Country X   Country Y

A = €33   Exports from A = €33 →   A = €33

B = €33   Exports from B = €33 ←   B = €33

Duopoly profit: €66   Duopoly profit: €66

This positive impact of import competition on prices does not only concern consumers; it will also benefit firms that use imported components. Indeed, if the opening to trade concerns intermediate products, the production costs of domestic firms that use imported components will fall; it will stimulate their exports and, therefore, employment.

Beyond its effect on prices, the opening up to imports will increase the variety of products. Imports give consumers access to a greater number of products. For example, the fact that France is open to international trade with Germany and Italy increases the number of top-of-the-range car models, compared to a situation of autarky.

Thus, in the case of European integration, the gain from trade between European countries is partly the result of an exchange of identical products of different quality (*intra-branch quality trade*).

The competitive effect of opening up to imports also translates into productivity gains. Domestic firms will react to the import shock by improving their efficiency or by being more innovative. Many empirical studies have thus shown that import competition stimulates innovation, especially in countries that were initially little exposed to competition (see Shu and Steinwender, 2019).

While a policy of trade liberalization improves welfare, it also has important redistributive effects at the domestic level.

On the losing side, we find industries that are competing with imports. They will reduce their level of production and their prices, which will result in job losses or wage cuts, as we saw in Chapter 3 on the U.S. case.

On the winning side, we find consumers of imported products – who pay less and have access to a greater variety of products – and exporting firms.

There is a fundamental asymmetry between the political weight of winners and losers. The losers, who are few in number, will organize themselves to prevent the opening up. Their weight and influence will be marked insofar as job losses are geographically concentrated. For example, the regions affected by import trade shocks are also those that express the strongest electoral preference for protectionist candidates. Dorn et al. (2017) have analyzed the results of the 2002 and 2010 U.S. congressional elections, as well as those of the 2000, 2008, and 2016 U.S. presidential elections. They found, well before the 2016 election of Donald Trump, a clear ideological shift in favor of protectionism in areas exposed to trade shocks.

For their part, the winners, who are numerous, will not be able to organize themselves to support free trade. Moreover, they are not really aware of the gains resulting from an opening to imports. Jaravel and Sager (2019) showed that each job destroyed in the United States because of Chinese competition created in return a $400,000 gain in purchasing power for the American economy. Who is aware of such an aggregate gain?

This asymmetry of forces logically leads political decision-makers to be very cautious about trade liberalization. They have to arbitrate between the interests of millions of consumers who vote little on economic issues and the interests of organized producers. This asymmetry is favorable to the maintenance of protectionism, as Vilfredo Pareto already pointed out in 1906 in his *Manual of Political Economy*: *"A protectionist measure brings large profits to a small number of people and causes a small amount of damage to a very large number of consumers. This circumstance makes it easier to put this protective measure into practice."* (free translation).

To make trade liberalization politically acceptable, governments can use two main levers:

– *Negotiate reciprocal trade liberalization between countries.* Job losses in the importing sectors will then be compensated by gains in market share and job creation in exports.

– *Accompany trade liberalization with a strong redistributive policy towards the losers.* The challenge is to compensate employees who have lost their jobs as a result of the opening up by, for example, financing their retraining.

IV. Opening Up Network Industries to Competition

As we saw in Chapter 3, when internal economies of scale are large in an industry, it is efficient for one firm to operate in the market.

This natural monopoly situation is found in industries such as gas, electricity, telecoms, and rail transport, which require the construction of expensive network infrastructure. For a long time, most countries chose to have a monopoly on infrastructure and services. This *legal monopoly* was present both upstream and downstream.

However, this vertically integrated monopoly scheme has been challenged since the 1980s in most developed countries. Indeed, the perimeter of the natural monopoly bears on the infrastructure and not the service. In fact, while it is inefficient to duplicate a network of oil pipelines, high-voltage lines, or railways, downstream competition in the service using these network infrastructures is possible (Figure 31).

The United Kingdom, since the 1980s, and the rest of Europe, since the 1990s, have gradually opened up their network industries to competition. In France, the opening up was organized according to a sectoral schedule: fixed-line phones (1998), electricity for large accounts (1999), gas for large accounts (2000), rail freight transport (2005), electricity and gas for individuals (2007), international passenger transport (2010), mail (2011), TER (2019), domestic TGV lines (2020), the bus network in the Ile-de-France region (2021), the bus network in Paris and the inner suburbs (planned for 2025), and the Paris metro and RER (planned for 2039).

Figure 31. Opening up the network industries to competition

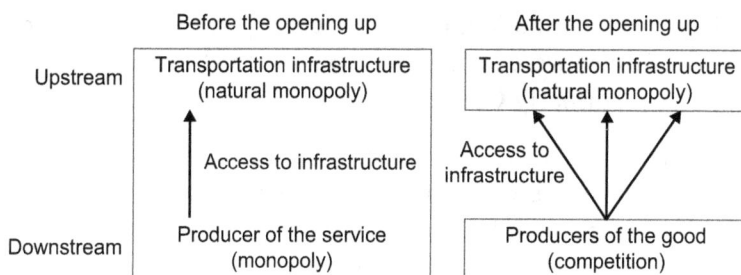

117

Opening up to competition requires a vertical separation between the network infrastructure (upstream), which remains a natural monopoly, and the service (downstream) that uses the network infrastructure and is open to new competitors.

Separating the infrastructure and the service has taken a more or less radical form between countries. In the United Kingdom, for example, in the rail sector, the choice was made to completely separate the two entities in order to avoid any conflict of interest. Thus, the rail network (rail and signaling) was privatized in 1994 and entrusted to Railtrack. Similarly, the national firm British Rail, which operated the train service through 25 regional firms, was privatized in 1996. Each regional entity was then assigned to a private operator through a competitive tender process. The private operator pays Railtrack a fee for using the rail network. It was less radical in other countries such as Italy and Germany, with a functional and accounting separation of the historical firm into two separate entities.

To illustrate this principle of separation between infrastructure and service, we can take the French example of electricity, gas, and rail (Table 12).

In the case of electricity, the infrastructure has been entrusted to RTE (a 50% subsidiary of EDF), which is in charge of the high-voltage line network, and to Enedis (a 100% subsidiary of EDF), for electricity distribution. For the electricity supply service, more than 30 suppliers were in competition in 2022, the main ones being EDF, Engie (formerly GDF), and Total Direct Energie.

In the case of gas, the infrastructure is entrusted to GRTGaz (a 75% subsidiary of Engie), which manages the gas pipeline network, and GRDF (an independent 100% subsidiary of Engie), which is in charge of the natural gas distribution network. The gas supply service has been opened up to competition: more than 15 operators were operating on the market in 2022, the main ones being Engie (ex-GDF), Total Direct Energie, and ENI.

In the case of trains, the historical firm SNCF remains a unified public group but is divided into two entities: SNCF Réseau for infrastructure and SNCF Voyageurs for train services. SNCF Réseau is responsible for charging tolls and allocating train paths to all railways companies. In order to avoid any conflict of interest, an "ethical wall" has been set between SNCF Group and SNCF Réseau: the directors of SNCF Réseau, appointed by the group, cannot participate in decisions concerning pricing and train-path allocation. This wall is important because the train service has been open to competition on high-speed lines since 2021 – the Italian operator Trenitalia has launched a high-speed train between Paris and Milan (via Lyon).

Table 12. The separation of infrastructure and service activities in France (gas, electricity, rail)

	Gas	Electricity	High-speed train
Infrastructure Network Operators	GRTGaz (gas pipelines) GRDF	RTE (high-voltage lines) Enedis	SNCF Réseau
Service operators (using the infrastructure)	Engie, Total Direct Energie, ENI, etc.	EDF, Engie, Total Direct Energie, etc.	SNCF Voyageurs Trenitalia

The service activity can be opened up to competition in two ways:

- *Competition for the market.* After an auction process, the market is awarded to the firm that offers the best price. For example, in the rail sector, France has chosen to allocate regional train services by tender; a single operator is awarded the contract, with public service obligations and financial compensation.

- *Competition in the market (open access).* Several operators can operate in the market simultaneously, as with gas, electricity, or telecoms today.

Operators' access to the infrastructure will be regulated by a tariff set in a transparent, objective, and non-discriminatory way. This tariff must enable the network company to finance the infrastructure and its maintenance.

The entire process of opening up and regulating competition is carried out under the aegis of an independent sectoral authority. Their role is to set the rules and foster new operators' entry. For example, in France, the Transport Regulation Authority (ART) ensures that all operators have fair access to the rail network. Among its central missions, it validates the setting of infrastructure fees relating to slots, rail station access, and rail security services.

Opening up the service to competition will have positive effects on the economy, as identified in Chapter 3: increased productivity, lower prices, increased volumes, and a positive impact on the quality of service.

As an example, in the case of passenger rail transport, the first assessment of the competitive reforms undertaken by some European countries on high-speed lines has been positive (see ART, 2018):

- Price reductions, sometimes significant, have been observed. In Italy, for example, the entry of a low-cost competitor (NTV) into the high-speed market in 2012 resulted in a significant reduction in the incumbent's ticket prices. In particular, the incumbent reduced its average ticket price on the Milan–Rome route by 30% between 2011 and 2012.

- Lower prices have strongly stimulated demand. For example, in Italy, the entry of a new operator in 2012 boosted ridership on high-speed rail services – between 2012 and 2015, the number of passengers increased by 49%.

- The quality of service, measured by objective indicators of user satisfaction, has improved significantly.

- Competition has led to the diversification of services. In Italy, for example, NTV sought to innovate in terms of quality of services on board by introducing free Wi-Fi, multimedia services, and top-of-the-range catering.

- Competition has not had a negative impact on rail safety, contrary to popular belief. The European countries that have opened up their market to competition in domestic passenger rail transport are among the safest in Europe. For example, over the past ten years, the United Kingdom and Germany have had few train accidents relative to their level of rail traffic.

However, the extent of these gains depends on the market share of newcomers. If we take the example of the railway, the situation is very different from one country to another in Europe. In the United Kingdom, new entrants have replaced the incumbent operator since the regional firms that have emerged from British Rail have been franchised. In other countries, given the high fixed costs of entry and the learning effect enjoyed by the incumbent firm, the market share of entrants appears to be more limited – in the rail sector, the market share is 30% in Germany, mainly on regional trains, and 20% in Italy, mainly on high-speed trains (Figure 32).

Figure 32. Market share of new entrants in the European railway sector

Taille du marché (en millions de trains-kilomètre)

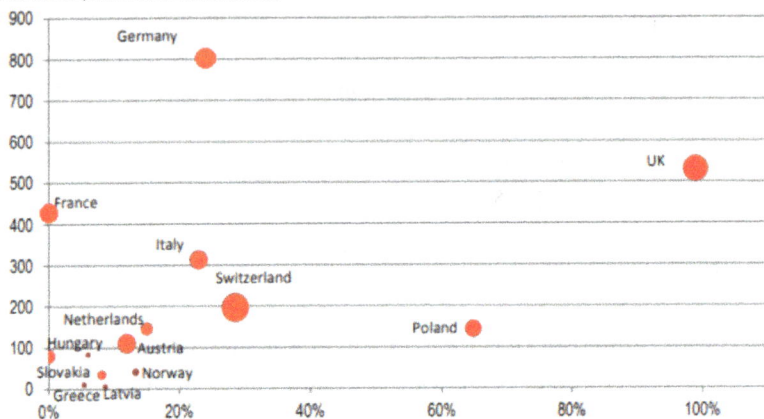

Part de marché des opérateurs alternatifs (non historiques) (en % de trains-km) - Source : IRG Rail

Source: ART (2018)

Chapter 6

The Role of Competition Policy

Pro-competitive policies are not just about opening up sectors to competition. They also consist of ensuring that firms do not artificially restrict competition with anti-competitive practices once the market has been opened up. This is the role assigned to competition policy, which originated in the United States at the end of the 19th century and has gradually spread to many countries.

The general principle underlying competition policy is that, by artificially curbing competition, anti-competitive practices have a negative effect on economic growth. The role of competition policy is therefore to detect and sanction these practices. If competition policy succeeds, firms will have no other choice to increase their profits than to be more efficient and innovative by engaging in "competition on the merits." Competition will result in productivity gains and economic growth. Buccirossi et al. (2013) have shown, on the basis of a sample of 12 OECD countries over the period spanning from 1995 to 2005, that the "tougher" a country's competition policy is (the severity being measured by the level of penalties), the higher its productivity (Figure 33).

Figure 33. The impact of competition policy on economic growth

Deterrent competition policy

↓

Incentives for incumbent firms to be efficient and innovative
(rather than collude, abuse their dominant position, or merge)

+

Entry of new competitors

↓

Productivity gains

↓

Economic growth

We will start by presenting the institutional framework of competition policy before addressing the issue of detection and punishment of anti-competitive practices, focusing on the specific case of cartels. We will conclude by analyzing the preventive role that competition policy plays through merger control.

I. The legal and institutional framework

Competition policy is governed by a specific legal framework – namely, competition law – composed of three main areas (Table 13).

The first area concerns horizontal and vertical agreements between firms aimed at "freezing competition." Schematically, agreements whose sole effect or object – like cartels – is to restrict trade are prohibited, while other forms of agreements are assessed according to a "rule of reason" (in the United States) or an exemption regime (in Europe). We will now focus on the particular case of cartels, whose harmful effects on the economy we saw in Chapter 3.

A second area deals with abuse of dominant position. We also saw in Chapter 3 that a dominant firm may have an incentive to exclude an equally efficient competitor or block its entry. The role of competition policy is to detect and sanction such practices, which can take different forms (see Combe, 2016; 2021). This policy is particularly difficult to implement – insofar as dominance itself is not prohibited – when it results from the firm's own merits (innovation, better quality of products, and so on). The aim of a competition policy is not to protect small, inefficient competitors, but to ensure that the dominant firm does not use its position to exclude as-efficient competitors.

The fight against anti-competitive agreements and abuses of dominant position is part of what we call *antitrust*. It involves punishing *ex post* individual (abuse of dominant position) or collective (agreement) practices that have harmed competition.

A third area concerns the control of mergers. Unlike antitrust, this policy intervenes before the merger is implemented. As we saw in Chapter 3, a merger may reduce the intensity of competition by reducing the number of firms in the market. This will result in a price increase, a reduction in products' quality, or incentive to innovate.

In addition to these three fundamental pillars of competition law, which are now found in many countries, Europe has developed a specific legislation on State aid. State aids are prohibited when they may distort competition within the European Union, and competition authorities must be notified in advance.

At the institutional level, competition policy is implemented mainly by competition authorities whose goal is to maintain the public economic order. In the case of the United States, competition policy is conducted by the U.S. Department of Justice (DOJ) through its Antitrust Division, and by a specialized agency – the Federal Trade Commission (FTC). At the European level, the European Commission is in charge of the competition policy through the Directorate General for Competition (DG Comp). The Commission does not have exclusive competence in the application of articles 101 and 102 of the Treaty on the Functioning of the European Union (TFEU), which is shared with the national competition authorities.

Table 13. The legal foundations of competition policy

Object	United States	European Union
Agreements	• Section 1 of the Sherman Act • Section 3 of the Clayton Act	Article 101 TFEU
Abuse of dominant position	• Section 2 of the Sherman Act • Section 2 of the Clayton Act (discrimination)	Article 102 TFEU
Merger control	• Section 7 of the Clayton Act • Celler-Kefauver Act • Hart-Scott-Rodino Act	Regulation 139/2004
State aid		Articles 107 and 108 TFEU

An important difference between European and American competition institutions is that in Europe, due to its supranational status, the Commission is relatively independent from Member States. European national governments defend the independence of the Commission because they fear that it could be influenced by another country (see Gutiérrez and Philippon, 2018). Conversely, in a country such as the United States, the agenda of competition authorities is more subject to political influences. For example, Philippon (2019) showed that in the United States during the 2000s, the money spent on lobbying and political campaign financing increased sharply and resulted in a "mothballing" of the antitrust authorities' action, particularly in the fight against abuse of dominance.

While antitrust agencies play the first role, competition policy can also be implemented by other institutions.

First, victims of anti-competitive practices can bring an action for compensation before a civil court. Although they are of a different legal nature than antitrust sanctions, claims for compensation increase the cost of infringement: the infringer will have not only to pay a fine (*public enforcement*) but also to compensate the victims (*private enforcement*). In the United States, civil actions represent the bulk of competition litigation at the federal level. Compensation amounts can be equivalent to or even exceed antitrust penalties The main challenge for victims is to quantify the damage they have suffered; they have to build the counterfactual situation *(but for)* that would have prevailed if the anti-competitive practice had not taken place.

Second, competition policy can take the form of criminal action against individuals who have taken part in the most serious anti-competitive practices: cartels. The country that really makes use of criminal prosecutions against individuals is the United States. The Sherman Act (1890), reinforced by the adoption in 2004 of the Antitrust Criminal Penalty Enhancement and Reform Act, provides for a penalty of up to $1 million and ten years in prison for individuals. This legal arsenal has been applied since the 1990s in major cartel cases.

II. The Fight Against Anti-Competitive Practices

The fight against cartels and abuses of dominant position presupposes that these practices can be detected effectively (1). Once detected, they must be sanctioned, which raises the issue of the effectiveness of sanctions (2).

1. A Difficult Detection

In the case of an abuse of a dominant position, it must be demonstrated that the practice is not the result of the firm's intrinsic superiority over its competitors. This demonstration is carried out in three steps.

The first step is to define the relevant market in which the firm operates. This step is often controversial: the firm claims a broad market definition in order to "dilute" a possible dominant position, while competition authorities often take a more restrictive approach. For example, in the 1992 *Kodak* case in the United States, the firm argued that the components of its photocopiers belonged to the broader market for photocopier components, regardless of the brand. However, the U.S. Supreme Court held that the relevant market was the market for components specific to Kodak copiers. Kodak therefore had a quasi-monopoly situation, although its overall market share for copiers would have been lower than 25%.

The second step consists of assessing the dominant position using a set of indicators, such as the market shares, the asymmetry of market shares, or the height of entry barriers.

If the firm is in a dominant position, the third step is to show that it has abused its position to exclude an *as-efficient competitor*. The abuse of a dominant position can take many forms, and it is usual to distinguish between tariff and non-tariff abuses:

- The main non-tariff abuses are tying, exclusive dealing, denial of access to essential infrastructure, or disparagement.

- The main tariff abuses are rebates, margin squeezes, and predatory pricing.

Competition authorities have repeatedly condemned dominant firms for abusing their positions, as in recent decisions in Europe (Table 14).

Table 14. Examples of abuse of dominant position

Case	Form of abuse	Fine
Microsoft (2004, EU)	The Commission accused Microsoft of eliminating competition in the market for media broadcasters by linking its Media Player product with its Windows operating system.	Penalty of €497 million (also for an abuse of the server operating system market). Microsoft is obliged to offer a version of Windows without Media Player.
Durogesic (2017, France)	Janssen-Cilag, owner of a patent on Durogesic, delayed the launch of Durogesic generics, in particular by spreading misleading messages to health professionals about the efficiency and safety of generics.	Sanction of €25 million.
Google (2018, EU)	The Commission concluded that Google engaged in two instances of illegal tying: • Google ensured its Google Search app was preinstalled on almost all Android devices. • Google ensured its mobile browser Chrome was preinstalled on almost all Android devices.	Sanction of €4.34 billion.
Qualcomm (2019, EU)	In the 3G baseband chipsets market, Qualcomm sold its chips at below-cost prices in order to foreclose its competitor Icera.	Sanction of €242 million.

In order to illustrate in a concrete way how an abuse can be detected, we can take the case of predatory pricing.

Predatory pricing is a strategy whereby a dominant firm first lowers its price in order to drive an equally efficient competitor out of the market. Once the competitor is out, the dominant firm then raises its price. This strategy is based on sacrificing profits in the short term, with the intent of recouping this loss in the long term.

Detecting a predatory price is a difficult task. It is necessary to distinguish a price cut motivated by the exclusion of an equally effective competitor from a price cut resulting from the competition. Indeed, a price cut, whether temporary or lasting, can have different causes:

- When demand in the market decreases, the price must adjust downwards if supply cannot decrease in the short term or if the products are difficult to stock.

- A decrease in the marginal cost of production (after a process innovation, for example) translates into a decrease in price.

- A firm trying to enter a new market may attract early clients by offering promotional prices. Similarly, a firm can temporarily sell its products at low prices when the learning curve is strong – a low price today allows the firm to sell in large quantities, which then reduces the unit cost of production.

- A temporary fall in prices may result from new competitors entering the market, leading to short-term overcapacity. In this case, incumbent firms will lower their prices in order to sell their production before the sector restructures (site closures, mergers, and so on).

To detect predatory pricing, antitrust authorities use a *cost test*, based on a comparison of the incumbent cost structure with the observed prices. The rule states that if the price is below the average variable cost, then there is a presumption of predatory behavior – it is not rational for a firm to sell an additional unit at a price below its variable cost.

Other evidence may also be used to demonstrate predatory pricing, including:

- *Asymmetries between firms.* For example, a multi-product or multi-market firm (think of a multinational) with market power can more easily support a price war if its competitor is a single-product or single-market firm.

- *The ability of the dominant firm to raise prices once the competitor has exited the market.*

- *Direct evidence of a predatory strategy, such as plans to drive a competitor out of business by temporarily lowering prices.*

In the case of secret practices such as cartels, detection is particularly difficult because cartel members will conceal evidence of their actions. In the elevator cartel case (2007), the European Commission noted that *"there is evidence that the companies were aware that their behaviour was illegal and they took care to avoid detection; they usually met in bars and restaurants, they travelled to the countryside or even abroad, and they used pre-paid mobile phone cards to avoid tracking"*.

Among the tools used to detect cartels, the so-called *leniency* policies play a key role. They consist of proposing to cartel members that they denounce the practice in which they take part in exchange for reductions/exemptions of penalties. In 2019, 60 countries worldwide operated cartel leniency programs, including emerging countries such as Brazil and China. Leniency policies have been quite successful. In the United States and Europe, more than 90% of the imposed penalties result from a leniency application.

Leniency policies have several objectives:

- They enable the detection of cartels that competition authorities would probably never have detected.

- They reduce the cost of detection when compared to traditional investigative methods, and allow cartel cases to be dealt with more quickly.

- They create instability within the cartels, with each member fearing denouncement by their partners.

- They deter firms from forming a cartel if they anticipate that the risk of denouncement is too great.

The effectiveness of a leniency policy depends on several factors, including:

- *The level of sanctions in the absence of a leniency program.* The more dissuasive the antitrust sanctions are, the more incentive there is for firms to apply for leniency.

- *The probability of detection in the absence of leniency.* If the probability is very low, firms have no interest in denouncing the practice. Therefore, it is important that antitrust authorities continue to investigate cartel cases so that firms consider the risk of detection credible.

- *The credibility and clarity of the leniency program.* Firms must be guaranteed sufficient legal certainty, particularly concerning the order of arrival and the amount of the penalty reduction.

- *The fine reduction for the first applicant and the difference between the first applicant and other cartel members.* Indeed, if the penalty reductions are small and uniform among cartel members, the latter will wait until competition authorities launch an investigation before cooperating. Conversely, leniency programs become very attractive if the first applicant can obtain total immunity from punishment and the others a small reduction (or even no reduction). The "first come, first served" principle is therefore essential to the success of leniency policies. In most countries, leniency programs provide a total exemption for the first applicant. In Europe, for example, in the truck cartel case, MAN escaped a penalty of €1.2 billion thanks to its cooperation with the European Commission, while other members of the cartel received a total penalty of €2.9 billion.

2. The Effectiveness of Sanctions

Once detected, anti-competitive practices must be punished with a financial penalty. In the case of cartels, the number of financial penalties in Europe has risen sharply since the 2000s, reflecting the increased severity of competition authorities (Figure 34).

Figure 34. Penalties imposed by the Commission on cartels (1990–2021; millions of euros)

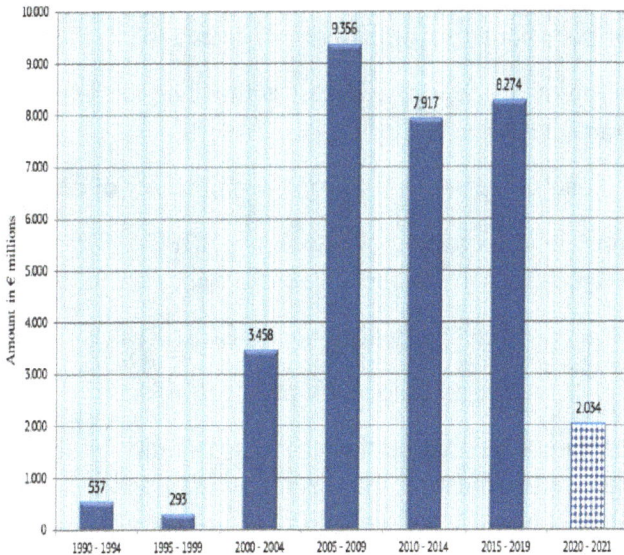

Source: DG Competition (2022)

133

The question that arises is how much monetary penalty should be imposed. The theory of *optimal sanctions*, inspired by the economics of crime (Becker, 1968), provides a powerful analytical framework to answer this question. A firm engages in an infringement by comparing the gains with the costs.

In the case of a cartel, the gain is the difference between the cartel price and the competitive price multiplied by the volume of transactions. In the case of an abuse of a dominant position, the gain also results from a higher price or a reduction in volumes for the competitors. The cost of infringement can be divided into two distinct elements: the amount of the penalty and the probability of being detected.

The firm does not violate the law if the expected cost of penalty exceeds the illicit gain, i.e.:

$$\text{expected cost of penalty} > \text{illegal gain}$$

$$\Leftrightarrow (\text{monetary penalty} \times \text{probability of detection}) > \text{illicit gain} \quad (1)$$

From the point of view of antitrust authorities, the amount of the penalty must be at least equal to:

$$\text{optimal monetary penalty} \geq (\text{illicit gain} / \text{probability of detection}) \quad (2).$$

For example, if the probability of detection is 20% (i.e., 0.2) and the illicit gain is €100, the optimal monetary penalty should be at least equal to:

$$\text{optimal monetary sanction} \geq €100 / 0.2$$

$$\text{optimal monetary penalty} \geq €500$$

We immediately see that the lower the probability of detection, the higher the penalty must be. The penalty must always be higher than the illicit gain, because the probability of detection is never 100%. In an abuse of dominant position, the probability of detection is probably higher than in a cartel, which is a secret practice.

Moreover, we find that the penalty has primarily a deterrent function; it is set in such a way that no firm will violate the law. The objective of an optimal sanction is not only to strongly punish those who are caught (individual deterrence) but also to send a message of general deterrence to firms that might be tempted to commit infringements.

There is a trade-off for antitrust authorities between the amount of the sanction and the detection rate. As detection is costly, the economic approach recommends setting low probabilities of detection with huge sanctions (compared to the illicit gain). However, this solution raises practical difficulties:

- Firms may not have the capability to pay huge sanctions.

- Penalties set at very high levels (because the probability of detection is low) imply that the firms caught "pay" for those not detected.

In reality, competition authorities use the two variables in a complementary manner, i.e., they act on both the amount and the probability of detection.

While it provides a powerful theoretical framework, the theory of optimal sanctions has several limitations when confronted with the practice of competition authorities. In particular, this approach does not take into account the intrinsic gravity of the practice, independent of its effects on the market. For example, cartels are sufficiently serious as to be condemned, whatever their effects.

Second, the criterion for determining financial penalties is the illicit gain. But an anti-competitive practice that raises prices also reduces demand. For example, a cartel does not only transfer surplus from consumers to producers; it also leads to a loss of welfare by reducing the quantities: if we consider that public action aims to protect consumer surplus, the sanction must include, in addition to the illicit gain, the loss of surplus.

III. Preventive Control of Mergers

In addition to its antitrust component, competition policy aims to prevent a merger from reducing competition, which would result in price increases, reduced quality, or reduced incentives to innovate. After briefly recalling the characteristics and outcomes of merger control (1), we will analyze the negative impact of a merger on competition and consider the role efficiencies play (2).

1. Merger Control: Characteristics and Outcomes

Merger control is based on the so-called *prior notification* system. Firms must seek approval before carrying out their projects. This system removes the uncertainty firms would face if control occurred after a completed merger. However, it is difficult for a competition authority to assess the effects of a merger before the merger has taken place. The risk for competition authorities is therefore twofold: to prohibit a merger that would have been pro-competitive (*type 1 error*) and to authorize a merger that will later turn out to be harmful to competition (*type 2 error*).

In many countries, merger control is mandatory as soon as the project exceeds certain thresholds, usually in terms of turnover. It applies in every jurisdiction where the firms are present, regardless of their nationality. For example, if two American firms decide to merge and make significant sales in the European market, they have to notify the European authorities. This situation leads to multiple notifications in the case of large mergers, and creates significant legal costs for firms.

To analyze the impact a merger will have on competition, the first step is to define the *relevant markets* – which products are on the same market as those of the merging firms? The aim is to assess the degree of substitutability between products. In practice, competition authorities use a set of indicators made up of qualitative and quantitative criteria. This exercise is delicate and often gives rise to divergent views between the competition authorities and the undertakings, which generally adopt a broad definition of the market in order to dilute their market share.

Once the relevant market has been defined, the second step is to assess the evolution of market shares after the merger. As a first approximation, the higher the market share of the merged firms, the more likely the new firm will obtain or strengthen its market power. It may also be useful to use a concentration index in order to estimate the impact the merger will have on all firms in the market, such as the Herfindahl-Hirschman Index (HHI), analyzed in Chapter 2.

These first two steps enable authorities to define *safety zones*, below which the merger is assumed not to harm competition significantly. For example, if the market share of the two firms after the merger is only 10%, it is highly unlikely that the merger will reduce competition.

Conversely, when market shares are significant, a proper competitive analysis of the transaction must be carried out.

As we saw in Chapter 4, in the case of a horizontal merger, there is a risk of price increase through a *unilateral* or *coordinated* effect. However, the risk may also concern other types of mergers, particularly vertical ones. Indeed, although the two merging firms are not competitors, there may be a competitive risk upstream or downstream. For example, if the merging firm controls access to a scarce resource upstream, it may restrict access to its competitors downstream (not vertically integrated).

For these anti-competitive risks to materialize, competition authorities must assess whether the market power of the new entity will not be countered by two factors:

- *The counterpower of consumers.* If there are few buyers (an oligopolistic situation), the impact of a merger on prices will be limited by the countervailing power of customers.

- *Barriers to entry.* If barriers are low, any attempt to raise prices after the merger will be thwarted by the entry of new firms. Competition authorities must therefore assess the extent of potential competition.

At the end of this merger's review, three types of decisions can be issued (Figure 35):

- *Unconditional acceptance.*

- *Conditional acceptance.* The merging firms must implement "remedies," such as selling certain assets to competitors. For example, in Bayer's 2018 takeover of Monsanto, the Commission conditioned the deal on the divestiture of a broad set of activities designed to remedy the overlaps in seeds, pesticides, and digital farming. In particular, Bayer's entire seed R&D activity was divested to a competitor.

- *Merger bans.* Decisions to ban are still rare, although they receive some media coverage. At the European level, from 2010 to 2021, a total of 10 bans were issued, representing less than 1% of notified cases. For example, in February 2019, the European Commission blocked the merger between Alstom and Siemens because the deal would have harmed competition in the markets for rail signaling systems and very high-speed trains in Europe.

Figure 35. Outcome of merger control in the European Union

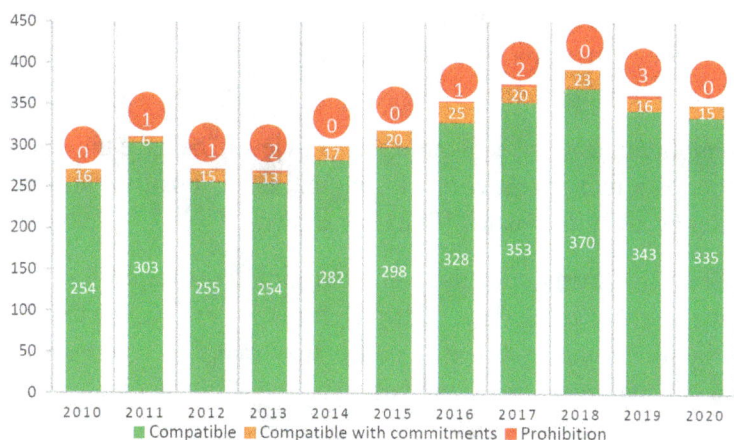

Source: European Commission (2021)

2. The Role of Efficiency Gains

While a merger can restrict competition, unlike a cartel, it can also generate efficiencies.

These efficiency gains have multiple origins and depend largely on the type of merger. For example, in the case of a merger between competitors, they may come from a reduction in the unit cost of production when the firms do not have the same technologies (productivity effect). The firm with the lowest costs will pass those costs on to the new entity. Similarly, a horizontal merger can create economies of scale. This phenomenon comes from fixed costs. When the level of production increases, fixed costs are spread over a larger quantity, which reduces the unit cost. Similarly, the increase in size allows for a better division of labor through task specialization. These economies of scale do not only occur in the production process; they can be extended to other functions such as distribution, marketing, or research and development.

It is important from an economic point of view to balance the negative effects of a merger on competition against its positive impact on efficiency, as Williamson (1968) has shown.

Suppose two firms with the same marginal cost (equal to c1) are competing over price (Figure 36). Before they merge, the two firms sell the total quantity Q1 at price P1: they make no profit since the price is equal to the marginal cost. The two firms decide to merge, which leads to a double effect:

- The marginal cost of production decreases from c1 to c2, thanks to efficiency gains.

- The price increases from P_1 to P_2, as the new entity is in a monopoly situation.

Before the merger, consumer surplus is equal to the area abd; since profits are zero, welfare (defined as the sum of profits and consumer surplus) is also equal to the triangle abd. After the merger, consumer surplus has decreased since consumers now pay more: consumers have lost the area (A + D). But the merger increases producer profit by an amount equal to the area (A + B). If we add the producers' gains to the consumers' losses (A + B − A − D), we obtain a final result equal to (B − D).

If B > D, the merger increases total welfare, although it reduces consumer surplus. Although the merger has eliminated all competition and penalized consumers (by increasing prices), welfare will increase because efficiency gains compensate for the loss of competition.

Figure 36. A merger that reduces competition but increases welfare

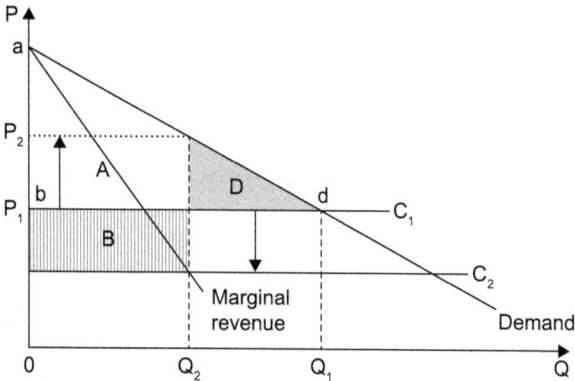

From a pure economic point of view, a merger should be accepted if it increases total welfare, even if it raises prices at the expense of consumers. In practice, however, competition authorities only take into account merger efficiencies if they benefit consumers, i.e., if they avoid price increases. This caution is explained by the fact that efficiencies are particularly difficult to estimate *ex ante*. Moreover, numerous empirical studies have shown a high failure rate in mergers and an overestimation of the expected gains: the value creation that should result from synergies between firms – summarized by the famous formula *1 + 1 = 3* – is often not achieved. A study by Blonigen and Pierce (2016) on a sample of mergers in the United States during the period spanning from 1997 to 2007 revealed that these operations had the effect of increasing margin rates, but that this effect resulted more from an increase in market power than from efficiency gains.

Conclusion

We opened this book with two famous quotes on competition – that of the liberal Frédéric Bastiat, who said that destroying competition "is to kill intelligence," and that of the libertarian anarchist Pierre-Joseph Proudhon, who said that "competition kills competition." In the light of economic theory and empirical tests, we can conclude that each of these statements contains some truth.

If competition is defined as a process by which new firms can continuously challenge incumbents' positions, then Bastiat is clearly right: competition is a form of economic democracy, allowing efficient firms to launch better products and services on the market. Competition is a permanent spur that eliminates unjustified rents. Moreover, it is not incompatible with a temporary monopoly situation or a dominant position acquired through merit (Chapter 2). In addition, the microeconomic and macroeconomic effects of competition, particularly after the entry of new firms into the market, can be extremely powerful, whether in terms of lower prices, quality, productivity gains, or innovation (Chapter 3).

But this definition of competition does not imply that competition is a self-sustaining process.

On the contrary, both economic theory and empirical studies show that the firm that dominates the market – initially on its own merits – may be tempted to maintain its market power by using anti-competitive practices. Different strategies can be implemented, such as cartels or abuse of dominant position (Chapter 4). The process of "creative destruction" can be blocked: competition will not only have killed less efficient competitors, it will also, to quote Proudhon, have "killed competition," without this being justified by the firm's own merits.

The role of the "visible hand" thus becomes central. Beyond the policies of opening up markets, the state's mission is to be a "market policeman," which detects and sanctions anti-competitive behaviors. In this respect, competition policy, and especially its antitrust component, plays a decisive role today (Chapter 6). More than 130 jurisdictions in the world now have competition laws and authorities that enforce them. There is also a legal arsenal at the international level to fight dumping or public subsidies that distort competition in international markets.

The challenge for competition policy is to find the right balance between the merits of firms and artificial rents. This debate is central today in sectors such as the digital economy, where firms often have large market shares. Some economists consider that these positions reflect digital firms' intrinsic superiority, favored by network effects that naturally lead to a dominant position (Chapter 4). Moreover, they consider that the dominant positions of GAFAM are fragile, insofar as they are not immune to disruptive innovation that would reshuffle the cards: in particular, the switching costs from one operator to another would be limited, especially if data portability measures are put in place. Competition would therefore be "just a mouse click away." On the other hand, other economists consider that GAFAM's dominant positions are also the result of anti-competitive strategies, leading to blocking new competitors.

More fundamentally, since competition is a permanent renewal process, it necessarily results in the creation and destruction of jobs (Chapter 3): new firms will come and take the place of other firms, leading to labor mobility within the sector and between sectors, but also geographically. Should we be concerned about this? Yes, insofar as workers' mobility is not instantaneous and is costly for individuals. Acquiring new skills takes time and geographical mobility is limited by transaction costs. In particular, we have seen that a rapid opening to international trade, such as the "Chinese shock," can impose strong adjustment costs on the importing country in the form of a lasting rise in unemployment in geographical areas affected by imported products.

Faced with this social cost, the temptation is great for the political decision-maker to opt for the status quo. He or she will obtain the support of firms that are reluctant to an opening up to competition. We have shown, by mobilizing the Olson paradox, how strong the resistance of the incumbent – who will put pressure on public authorities to maintain or reinforce the restrictions on competition – can be (Chapter 5). But restricting competition is ultimately costly for growth, as it limits productivity gains and innovation.

The key issue is therefore how to combine the virtuous effects of competition in the product market with the necessary protection of the people in the labor market. Competition is only socially acceptable if it benefits everyone.

Index

A

B

C

D

Bibliography

Acemoglu, D., Autor, D., Dorn, D., Hanson, G., and Price, B. (2016) "Import competition and the Great U.S. Employment Sag of the 2000s," *Journal of Labor Economics*, 34(S1), pp. S141–S198.

Aghion, P., Harris, C., Howitt, P., and Vickers, J. (2001) "Competition, imitation and growth with step-by-step innovation," *Review of Economic Studies*, 68, pp. 476–492.

Aghion, P., Bloom, N., Blundell, R., Griffith, R., and Howitt, P. (2005) "Competition and innovation: An inverted-U relationship," *The Quarterly Journal of Economics*, 2, pp. 701–728.

Aghion, P., Blundell, R., Griffith, R., Howitt, P., and Prantl, S. (2009) "The effects of entry on incumbent innovation and productivity," *The Review of Economics and Statistics*, 91 (1), pp. 20–32.

Aghion, P. and Howitt, P. (2010) *L'économie de la croissance*, Economica.

Aghion, P., Antonin, C., and Bunel, S. (2020) *Le pouvoir de la destruction créatrice*, Odile Jacob.

Aghion, P., Benabou, R., Martin, R., and Roulet, A. (2021) "Environmental Preferences and Technological Choices: Is Market Competition Clean or Dirty?," *Working Paper Collège de France*, 36 p.

Arrow, K. (1962) "Economic Welfare and the Allocation of Resources for Invention," in R. Nelson (ed.) *The Rate and Direction of Inventive Activity*, Princeton University Press.

Ashenfelter, O. and Krueger, A. (2018) "Theory and evidence on employer collusion in the franchise sector," *NBER Working paper* no. 24831, 29 pp.

Askenazy, P. and Weidenfeld, K. (2007) *Les soldes de la Loi Raffarin: Le Contrôle du Commerce Alimentaire*, Presses de l'ENS.

ART (2018) *The opening of passenger rail transport to competition in France: European lessons.*

Ater, I. and Rigbi, O. (2017) "The Effects of Mandatory Disclosure of Supermarket Prices," *Working Paper SSRN*, 45 pp.

Autor, D., Dorn, D., and Hanson, G. (2013) "The China Syndrome: Local Labor-Market Effects of Import Competition in the United States," *American Economic Review*, 103(6), pp. 2121–2168.

Autor, D., Dorn, D., and Hanson, G. (2016) "The China Shock: Learning from Labor-Market Adjustment to Large Changes in Trade," *Annual Review of Economics*, 8, pp. 205–240.

Autor, D., Dorn, D., Kratz, L. F., Patterson, C., and Van Reenen J. (2019) "The Fall of the Labor Share and the Rise of Superstar Firms," *Quarterly Journal of Economics*, 135(2), pp. 645–709.

Azar, J., Marinescu, I., and Steinbaum, M. (2017) "Labor market concentration," *NBER Working Paper* No. 24147.

Azar, J., Huet-Vaughn, E., Marinescu, I., Taska, B., and Von Wachter, T. (2019) "Minimum Wage Employment Effects and Labor Market Concentration," *Working paper SSRN*, 39 pp.

Bambalaite, I., Nicoletti, G., and Von Rueden, C. (2020) "Occupational Entry Regulations and Their Effects on Productivity in Services: Measurement and Firm-Level Evidence," *OECD Economics Department Working Papers*, No. 1605, Paris.

Bain, J. (1956) *Barriers to New Competition*, Cambridge University Press.

Bajari, P., Chernozhukov, V., Hortaçsu A., and Suzuki, J. (2018) "The Impact of Big Data on Firm Performance: An Empirical Investigation" *NBER Working Paper* No. 24334, 72 pp.

Bajgar, M., Berlingieri, G., Calligaris, S., Criscuolo, C., and Timmis, J. (2019) "Industry Concentration in Europe and North America," *OECD Productivity Working Papers*, No. 18.

Barone, G. and Cingano, F. (2011) "Service regulation and growth: Evidence from OECD countries," *Economic Journal*, 121(555), pp. 931–957.

Bartelsman, E., Haltiwanger, J., and Scarpetta, S. (2004) "Microeconomic Evidence of Creative Destruction in Industrial and Developing Countries," IZA discussion paper.

Basker, E. (2005) "Job creation or destruction? Labor-market effects of Walmart expansion," *Review of Economics and Statistics*, 87(1), pp. 174–183.

Bastiat, F. (1851) *Les Harmonies économiques*, Guillaumin, 2nd edition.

Baumol, W., Panzar, J., and Willig, R. (1982) *Contestable Markets and the Theory of Industry Structure*, Harcourt Brace Jovanovich.

Becker, G. (1968) "Crime and punishment: An economic approach," *Journal of Political Economy*, 76(169), pp. 169–217.

Ben Hassine, H. (2019) "Productivity growth and resource reallocation in France: The process of creative destruction," *Économie et Statistique*, 507 (1), pp. 115–133.

Benmelech, E., Bergman, N., and Hyunseob, K. (2018) "Strong Employers and Weak Employees: How Does Employer Concentration Affect Wages?" *NBER Working Paper* No. 24307, 51 pp.

Bertrand, J. (1883) "Revue de la théorie mathématique de la richesse sociale," *Journal des Scholars*, pp. 499–508.

Bertrand, M. and Kramarz, F. (2002) "Does entry regulation hinder job creation? Evidence from the French retail industry," *Quarterly Journal of Economics*, 117(14), pp. 1369–1414.

Blanchard, O. and Giavazzi, F. (2003) "Macroeconomic Effects of Regulation and Deregulation in Goods and Labor Markets," *The Quarterly Journal of Economics*, 118(3), pp. 879–907.

Blonigen, B. and Pierce, J. (2016) "Evidence for the Effects of Mergers on Market Power and Efficiency," *Board of Governors of the Federal Reserve System*, No. 82.

Bork, R. (1973) *The Antitrust Paradox: A Policy at War with Itself*, Free Press.

Bourlès, R., Cette, G., Lopez, J., Mairesse, J., and Nicoletti, G. (2013) "Do product market regulations in upstream sectors curb productivity growth? Panel data evidence for OECD countries," *The Review of Economics and Statistics*, pp. 1750–1768.

Bourreau, M., Sun, Y., and Verboven, F. (2018) "Market entry, fighting brands and tacit collusion: The case of the French mobile telecommunications market," Working Paper, 45 pp.

Boyer, M. and Kotchoni, R. (2015) "How much do cartels overcharge?," *Review of Industrial Organization*, 47(2), pp. 119–153.

Bridgman, B., Gomes, V., and Teixeria, A. (2011) "Threatening to Increase Productivity: Evidence from Brazil's Oil Industry," *World Development*, 39(8) pp. 1372–1385.

Brown, A. (2017) "The effects of airline behavior on aircraft accidents," *The Gettysburg Economic Review*, 10(1), pp. 70–105.

Brown, J. and Goolsbee, A. (2002) "Does the Internet make markets more competitive? Evidence from the life insurance industry," *Journal of Political Economy*, 110(3) pp. 481–507.

Buccirossi, P., Ciari, L., Duso, T., Spagnolo, G., and Vitale, C. (2013) "Competition policy and productivity growth: An empirical assessment," *The Review of Economics and Statistics*, 95(4), pp. 1323–1336.

Burnham, T., Frels, J., and Mahajan, V. (2003) "Consumer switching costs: A typology, antecedents, and consequences," *Journal of the Academy of Marketing Science*, 31, pp. 109–126.

Cahuc, P., Kramarz, F., and Zylberberg, A. (2006) "Les ennemis de la concurrence et de l'emploi," *Commentaires* pp. 389–405.

Castanheira, M., Ornaghi, C., and Siotis, G. (2019) "The unexpected consequences of generic entry," *Journal of Health Economics*, 68, pp. 268–285.

Cavallo, A. (2018) "More Amazon Effects: Online Competition and Pricing Behaviors," *NBER Working Paper* No. 25138, 37 pp.

CEPII (2013) "(Not) Made in France," *Lettre du CEPII*, no. 333.

Cette, G., Lopez, J., and Mairesse, J. (2018) "Rent Creation and Sharing: New Measures and Impacts on TFP," *NBER Working Paper* No. 24426.

CMA (2015) *Productivity and Competition: A Summary of the Evidence*, report.

Combe, E. (2014) *Le low cost: une révolution économique et démocratique*, Fondapol, 56 p.

Combe, E. (2016) *La politique de la concurrence*, Repères/La Découverte, 128 pp.

Combe, E. (2019) *Towards Personalized Prices?*, Fondapol, 38 pp.

Combe, E., Hyppolite, A., and Michon, A. (2019) *Europe in the Age of American and Chinese Nationalism*, Fondapol, 3 vols.

Combe, E. (2021) *Competition Policy: An Empirical and Economic Approach*, Wolters Kluwer.

Combe, E. and Monnier, C. (2012) "Les cartels en Europe: une analyse empirique," *Revue française d'économie*, pp. 1–40

Cournot, A. (1838) *Recherches sur les principes mathématiques de la théorie des richesses*, Hachette.

Covarrubias, M., Gutiérrez, G., and Philippon, T. (2019) "From Good to Bad Concentration? U.S. Industries Over the Past 30 years," *NBER Working Paper*, No. 25983.

Cunningham, C., Ma, S., and Ederer, F. (2018) "Killer Acquisitions," *Academy of Management proceedings*.

De Loecker, J., Eeckhout, J., and Unger, G. (2020) "The rise of market power and the macroeconomic implications," *The Quarterly Journal of Economics*, 135(2), pp. 561–644.

Delpla, J. and Wyplosz, C. (2007) *La fin des privilèges: payer pour réformer*, Hachette.

Direction Générale du Trésor (2009) "Competition and productivity gains: A sectoral analysis in OECD countries," *Trésor-Economics*, No. 51.

Dorn, D., Hanson, G., and Majlesi, K. (2017) "Importing Political Polarization? The Electoral Consequence of Rising Trade Exposure," *NBER Working Paper* No. 22637.

Colvin, A. and Shierholz, H. (2019) "Noncompete Agreements," Economic Policy Institute Report, 16 pp.

Ezrachi, A. and Stucke, M. (2016) *Virtual Competition*, Harvard University Press.

Fabrizio, K., Rose, N., and Wolfram, C. (2007) "Do markets reduce costs? Assessing the impact of regulatory restructuring on U.S. electric generation efficiency," *American Economic Review*, 97(4), pp. 1250–1277.

Farronato, C., Fradkin, A., Larsen, B., and Brynjolfsson, E. (2020) "Consumer Protection in an Online World: An Analysis of Occupational Licensing," *NBER Working Paper* No. 26601, 72 pp.

Fang, H., Wang, L., and Yang, Y. (2020) "Competition and Quality: Evidence from High-Speed Railways and Airlines," *NBER Working Paper* No. 27475.

Feenstra, R., Ma, H., and Xu, Y. (2017) "U.S. Exports and Employment," *NBER Working Paper* No. 24056.

Feenstra, R. and Sasahara, A. (2017) "The 'China Shock,' Exports and U.S. Employment: A Global Input-Output Analysis," *NBER Working Paper* No. 24022.

Flaaen, A., Hortaçsu, A., and Tintelnot, F. (2019a) "The Production, Relocation and Price Effects of U.S. Trade Policy: The Case of Washing Machines," *FI Working Paper*.

Flaaen, A. and Pierce, P. (2019b) "Disentangling the Effects of the 2018–2019 Tariffs on a Globally Connected U.S. Manufacturing Sector," *Board of Governors of the Federal Reserve System.*

Foster, L., Haltiwanger, J., and Krizan, C. J. (2001) "Aggregate productivity growth: Lessons from microeconomic evidence," in Dean, Herper, Hulten (ed) *News Developments in Productivity Analysis*, University of Chicago Press.

Furman, J., Russ, K., and Shambaugh, J. (2017) "U.S. tariffs are an arbitrary and regressive tax," *VOX/CEPR*, 12 January.

Furman, J. (2019) *Unlocking Digital Competition: Report from the Digital Competition Expert Panel*, report.

Greenfield, D. (2014) "Competition and air service quality: New evidence from the airline industry," *Economics of Transportation*, 3(1), pp. 80–89.

Grullon, G., Larkin, Y., and Michaely, R. (2019) "Are U.S. industries becoming more concentrated?," *Review of Finance*, 23(4), pp. 697–743.

Gutiérrez, G. and Philippon, T. (2018), "How EU Markets Became More Competitive than U.S. Markets: A Study of Institutional Drift," *NBER Working Paper*, No. 24700.

Hayek, F. (1948) "The meaning of competition," in *Individualism and Economic Order*, University of Chicago Press.

Hicks, J. (1935) "The theory of monopoly," *Econometrica*, pp. 1–20.

Hufbauer, G. and Kimberly, E. (1994) *Measuring the Costs of Protection in the United States*, Institute for International Economics.

Hufbauer, G. and Lowry, S. (2012) *U.S. Tire Tariffs: Saving Few Jobs at High Cost*, Peterson Institute for International Economics, No. 12.

Jaravel, X. and Sager, E. (2019) "What are the Price Effects of Trade? Evidence from the U.S. and Implications for Quantitative Trade Models," *Finance and Economics Discussion Series*, Board of Governors of the Federal Reserve System.

Khan, L. (2016) "Amazon's antitrust paradox," *The Yale Law Journal*, 126(3), pp. 710–805.

Kleiner, M. and Krueger, A. (2010) "The prevalence and effects of occupational licensing," *British Journal of Industrial Relations*, 48(4), pp. 676–687.

Krueger, A. (1974) "The political economy of the rent-seeking society," *American Economic Review*, 64(3), pp. 291–303.

Laffont, J. J. and Tirole, J. (2012) *Théorie des incitations et réglementation*, Economica.

Levêque, F. (2017) *Les habits neufs de la concurrence*, Odile Jacob.

Malmendier, U. and DellaVigna, S. (2006) "Paying not to go to the gym," *American Economic Review*, 96(3), pp. 694–719.

Matsa, D. (2009) "Competition and product quality in the supermarket industry," Working Paper, Northwestern University.

Mazzeo, M. (2003) "Competition and service quality in the U.S. airline industry," *Review of Industrial Organization*, 22, pp. 275–296.

McGee, J. (1971) *In Defense of Industrial Concentration*, Praeger Publishers.

Morrison, S. A. (2001) "Actual, adjacent, and potential competition: Estimating the full effect of Southwest Airlines," *Journal of Transport Economics and Policy*, 35(2), pp. 239–256.

Motta, M. (2004) *Competition Policy: Theory and Practice*, Cambridge University Press.

Naidu, S., Posner, E., and Weyl, E. G. (2018) "Antitrust remedies for labor market power," *Harvard Law Review*, 132(2), pp. 537–601.

OECD (2018) *Product market regulation*, Paris.

OECD (2019a) *OECD Economic Surveys: France*, Paris.

OECD (2019b) *Competition concerns in labor markets*, Paris.

OECD (2020) *Measuring occupational entry regulations: A new OECD approach*, Working paper No. 1606, Paris.

Philippon, T. (2019) *The Great Reversal: How America Gave Up On Free Markets*, Harvard University Press.

Proudhon, J. (1846) *Système des contradictions économiques ou Philosophie de la misère*, Garnier.

Dallas Federal Reserve (2002) *The fruits of free trade*, annual report.

Rose, N. (1987) "Labor rent sharing and regulation: Evidence from the trucking industry," *Journal of Political Economy*, 95(6), pp. 1146–1178.

Schmitz, J. (2005) "What determines productivity? Lessons from the dramatic recovery of the U.S. and Canadian iron ore industries following their early 1980s crisis," *Journal of Political Economy*, 113(3), pp. 582–625.

Schumpeter, J. (1911) *Theory of Economic Evolution*, French translation of 1935, Payot.

Schumpeter, J. (1943) *Capitalism, Socialism and Democracy*, 1951 French translation, Payot.

Scott Morton, F., Zettelmeyer, F., and Silva-Risso, G. (2003) "Internet car retailing," *Journal of Industrial Economics*, 49 (4), pp. 501–519.

Sraer, D. (2010) *Les vertus de la concurrence*, Fondapol.

Stigler, G. (1961) "The economics of information," *The Journal of Political Economy*, 69 (3), pp. 213–225.

Shu, P. and Steinwender, C. (2019) "The Impact of Trade Liberalization on Firm Productivity and Innovation," *Innovation Policy and the Economy*, University of Chicago Press, vol. 19(1), pp. 39–68.

Syverson, C. (2019) Macroeconomics and market power: Facts, potential explanations, and open questions, *Journal of Economic Perspectives*, pp. 23–43.

Tirole, J. (2015) *Theory of Industrial Organization*, Economica.

Tirole, J. (2016) *Économie du bien commun*, PUF.

Tirole, J. (2020) "Competition and the industrial challenge for the digital age," *Document de TSE work*, 29 p.

UFC Que choisir (2014) *Concurrence dans la téléphonie mobile: Un bilan sans appel*, Service des études, 50 p.

Wallsten, S. (2015) "The competitive effects of the sharing economy: How is Uber changing taxis?" *Working paper Technology Policy Institute.*

Williamson, O. (1968), "Economies as an antitrust defense: The welfare tradeoffs," *American Economic Review*, 58, pp. 18–36.

The Institute of Competition Law

The Institute of Competition Law is a publishing company, founded in 2004 by Dr. Nicolas Charbit, based in Paris, London and New York. The Institute cultivates scholarship and discussion about antitrust issues though publications and conferences. Each publication and event is supervised by editorial boards and scientific or steering committees to ensure independence, objectivity, and academic rigor. Thanks to this management, the Institute has become one of the few think tanks in Europe to have significant influence on antitrust policies.

AIM

The Institute focuses government, business and academic attention on a broad range of subjects which concern competition laws, regulations and related economics.

BOARDS

To maintain its unique focus, the Institute relies upon highly distinguished editors, all leading experts in national or international antitrust: Bill Kovacic, Mario Monti, Eleanor Fox, Laurence Idot, Frédéric Jenny, Ioannis Lianos, Richard Whish, etc.

AUTHORS

4,000 authors, from 85 jurisdictions.

PARTNERS

- Universities: University College London, King's College London, Queen Mary University, Paris Sorbonne Panthéon-Assas, etc.

- Law firms: Allen & Overy, Cleary Gottlieb Steen & Hamilton, Baker McKenzie, Hogan Lovells, Jones Day, Norton Rose Fulbright, Skadden Arps, White & Case, etc.

EVENTS

Brussels, Dusseldorf, Hong Kong, London, Milan, New York, Paris, Singapore, Warsaw and Washington DC.

ONLINE VERSION

Concurrences website provides all articles published since its inception.

PUBLICATIONS

The Institute publishes Concurrences Review, a print and online quarterly peer-reviewed journal dedicated to EU and national competitions laws. e-Competitions is a bi-monthly antitrust news bulletin covering 85 countries. The e-Competitions database contains over 24,000 case summaries from 4,000 authors.

Concurrences
Competition Laws Review

Concurrences Review

Concurrences is a print and online quarterly peer reviewed journal dedicated to EU and national competitions laws. It has been launched in 2004 as the flagship of the Institute of Competition Law in order to provide a forum for academics, practitioners and enforcers. Concurrences' influence and expertise has garnered contributions or interviews with such figures as Christine Lagarde, Bill Kovacic, Emmanuel Macron, Antonin Scalia and Magrethe Vestager.

CONTENTS

More than 14,000 articles, print and/or online. Quarterly issues provide current coverage with contributions from the EU or national or foreign countries thanks to more than 2,500 authors in Europe and abroad.

FORMAT

In order to balance academic contributions with opinions or legal practice notes, Concurrences provides its insight and analysis in a number of formats:

- Forewords: Opinions by leading academics or enforcers
- Interviews: Interviews of antitrust experts
- On-Topics: 4 to 6 short papers on hot issues
- Law & Economics: Short papers written by economists for a legal audience
- Articles: Long academic papers
- Case Summaries: Case commentary on EU and French case law
- Legal Practice: Short papers for in-house counsels
- International: Medium size papers on international policies
- Books Review: Summaries of recent antitrust books
- Articles Review: Summaries of leading articles published in 45 antitrust journals

BOARDS

The Scientific Committee is headed by Laurence Idot, Professor at Panthéon Assas University. The International Committee is headed by Frederic Jenny, OECD Competition Comitteee Chairman. Boards members include Douglas Ginsburg, Benoît Cœuré, Howard Shelanski, Richard Whish, Wouter Wils, Joshua Wright, etc.

ONLINE VERSION

Concurrences website provides all articles published since its inception, in addition to selected articles published online only in the electronic supplement.

WRITE FOR CONCURRENCES

Concurrences welcome spontaneous contributions. Except in rare circumstances, the journal accepts only unpublished articles, whatever the form and nature of the contribution. The Editorial Board checks the form of the proposals, and then submits these to the Scientific Committee. Selection of the papers is conditional to a peer review by at least two members of the Committee. Within a month, the Committee assesses whether the draft article can be published and notifies the author.

e-Competitions Bulletin

CASE LAW DATABASE

e-Competitions is the only online resource that provides consistent coverage of antitrust cases from 85 jurisdictions, organized into a searchable database structure. e-Competitions concentrates on cases summaries taking into account that in the context of a continuing growing number of sources there is a need for factual information, i.e., case law.

- 24,000 case summaries
- 4,000 authors
- 85 countries covered
- 30,000 subscribers

SOPHISTICATED EDITORIAL AND IT ENRICHMENT

e-Competitions is structured as a database. The editors make a sophisticated technical and legal work on all articles by tagging these with key words, drafting abstracts and writing html code to increase Google ranking. There is a team of antitrust lawyers – PhD and judges clerks – and a team of IT experts. e-Competitions makes comparative law possible. Thanks to this expert editorial work, it is possible to search and compare cases by jurisdiction, legal topics or business sectors.

PRESTIGIOUS BOARDS

e-Competitions draws upon highly distinguished editors, all leading experts in national or international antitrust. Advisory Board Members include: Sir Christopher Bellamy, Ioanis Lianos (UCL), Eleanor Fox (NYU), Frédéric Jenny (OECD), Jacqueline Riffault-Silk (Cour de cassation), Wouter Wils (King's College London), etc.

LEADING PARTNERS

- Association of European Competition Law Judges: The AECLJ is a forum for judges of national Courts specializing in antitrust case law. Members timely feed e-Competitions with just released cases.

- Academics partners: Antitrust research centres from leading universities write regularly in e-Competitions: University College London, King's College London, Queen Mary University, etc.

- Law firms: Global law firms and antitrust niche firms write detailed cases summaries specifically for e-Competitions: Allen & Overy, Baker McKenzie, Cleary Gottlieb Steen & Hamilton, Jones Day, Norton Rose Fulbright, Skadden, White & Case, etc.

19 years of archives
30,000 articles

4 DATABASES

Concurrences
Access to latest issue and archives

- 14,000 articles from 2004 to the present
- European and national doctrine and case law

e-Competitions
Access to latest issue and archives

- 24,000 case summaries from 1911 to the present
- Case law of 85 jurisdictions

Books
Access to all Concurrences books

- 70 e-Books available
- PDF version

Conferences
**Access to the documentation
of all Concurrences events**

- 600 conferences (Brussels, Hong Kong, London, New York, Paris, Singapore and Washington, DC)
- 350 PowerPoint presentations, proceedings and syntheses
- 550 videos
- Verbatim reports

NEW

New search engine
Optimized results to save time

- Search results sorted by date, jurisdiction, keyword, economic sector, author, etc.

New modes of access
IP address recognition

- No need to enter codes: immediate access
- No need to change codes when your team changes: offers increased security and saves time

Mobility
- Responsive design: site optimized for tablets and smartphones